CHRI

CHRIST

and

BAHÁ'U'LLÁH

by

GEORGE TOWNSHEND, M.A.
(Sometime Canon of St. Patrick's Cathedral, Dublin
Archdeacon of Clonfert)

GEORGE RONALD
Oxford

Printed in Great Britain at the Alden Press, Oxford

I wish to acknowledge my debt to my dear son and daughter, Brian and Una, for their devotion, high enthusiasm and their manifold helpfulness in the writing of this book.

GEORGE TOWNSHEND.

CONTENTS

The Bahá'í Faith is now (1990) represented in 168 independent countries and 49 dependent territories or overseas departments; its literature has been translated into over 800 languages. These figures correct those on p.116.

PROLOGUE

BRIEFLY but clearly, and with all possible emphasis, facts are given in this little book to prove that the Kingdom of God, as foretold in the Bible with a thousand details, has at last come with those details all fulfilled.

In all the revealed world religions the coming of the Kingdom is identified with the appearance of the Supreme World Redeemer, the Lord of Hosts, the returned Christ, the Qá'im, the new Buddha. "*One fold and one shepherd*" is to replace the many conflicting and separated groups of men.

This outstanding pledge, originally given thousands of years ago, has never been taken up by any of the Great Prophets until the nineteenth century, when Bahá'u'lláh, Founder of the Bahá'í Faith, announced to the rulers and religious leaders of the world that He was this Redeemer and the Bearer of God's message to modern man. He proclaimed that He spoke with the Voice of God Himself, that He was the Lord of Hosts, Christ come in the glory of the Father, and that this was indeed the Last Day, the Day of Judgment. The Cause of Bahá'u'lláh and His martyred Forerunner, the Báb, had for twenty years suffered persecution of every form; yet without investigation the kings and ecclesiastical rulers whom He addressed ignored His message. He died in 1892 in the Holy Land, an exile and captive of the Turks. Yet to-day a world-wide community exists bearing His name and following His teachings.

Twentieth century thought and aspiration are deeply committed to the social and humanitarian principles which Bahá'u'lláh announced, though His spiritual message is, as yet, ignored and certainly no relationship is conceived between the idea of world order and the Kingdom of God.

This book is directed especially to the Christians whose age-long prayer, given by Christ Himself, is *"Thy kingdom come"*. Unfortunately the Christian Churches are in disagreement as to what this means and they are, therefore, powerless to meet the crisis of our times.

The message of Bahá'u'lláh opens to Christians the one door leading to the certain prospect of fulfilment of all that is best in their great tradition, the fairest hope of service and of redemption in the future.

Chapter One

GOD'S CALL TO THE CHRISTIANS

G OD has ordained that the Christians of the West shall be foremost among all the peoples of the world in recognizing and acknowledging the second coming of Christ in the glory of the Father and in carrying the glad tidings through the earth.[1]

The Kingdom of God has come! The Lord of Hosts has appeared with all the prophesied tokens! His teachings have gone through the earth and He has proclaimed His message to the kings and religious leaders. But the Christians hesitate, the churches will not acknowledge nor even investigate. They do not heed nor understand the prophetic outline which Christ in Palestine gave to the disciples on the nature of the first Christian era—the period between the first and second coming—and of the special dangers and difficulties which would beset the Church during the whole of that time. He declared that there would be no certain knowledge of Christian truth in those centuries, no agreement, but endless doubt and dispute and difficulty. The enemies of the Church would not be open and notorious foes but would be within its own ranks. The Christian community, He warned them, would be like a ripening cornfield, infested with masses

---

[1] Bahá'u'lláh, *Tablet to Napoleon III*.
Shoghi Effendi, *America & The Most Great Peace*.

of weeds growing so close and strong they could not be dug out but would have to be left to do their evil work right through to the harvest time.[1] Then they would reach their highest point. The typical enemy of the Church would be the false prophet who would pervert the true meaning of the Gospel and would mystify people's minds so cunningly that he might even deceive the very elect, at the last, at harvest, when the reapers would gather the weeds, bind them in bundles and burn them.[2] The teaching position would become so bad that men would fear the gates of hell might prevail against the true doctrine. Christ reassured His little flock, bade them not fear because it was their Father's good pleasure to give them the Kingdom.

The Christians of to-day and yesterday have not noticed the accuracy of Christ's forecast, nor do they see that the very things of which Christ warned them are happening to-day.

Now the promised change has come. This is the time which Christ foresaw when He affirmed that He had many more things to tell the disciples but He must withhold them because they were not mature enough to bear them. At last the age of maturity has been reached. The time of uncertainty and doubt, of self-delusion and idle fancy and vain imaginings has gone by. The "Spirit of Truth" has come. A new heaven and a new earth are spread before mankind and every man is required to "prove all things" and "hold fast that which is good".

This book is written lest Christian men and women, confused by past errors and falsities, should neglect to observe the newness of the age, to heed the warnings of

[1] *Matt.* xiii 24-30.
[2] *Mark* xiii 22. *Matt.* xxiv 24.

Christ and should fall into the snare of which He told them all so often and so emphatically. Let them not, through lack of discernment or courage, play into the hands of those who are bringing destruction.

This book is written to prove, from the undoubted facts of history, what is the true interpretation of Jesus' prophecies about the character of His era, to show the justice of His warnings, especially at this time when the events He foretold have reached the crisis of their fulfilment.

May the Father, in His mercy, grant that the Christians of the West may be shaken out of their composure, may be moved before it is too late to investigate the truth and may at last arise to meet the tremendous, unprecedented emergency which opens before them.

CHAPTER TWO

THE KINGDOM IN THE BIBLE

THE story of the coming of the Kingdom runs through the whole Bible. It is the climax and consummation of God's grand redemptive scheme. The attainment of the Kingdom at the end is promised in the beginning, and gives to the Bible its note of confident expectation, of success and triumph.

Jesus made mention of Noah and Abraham as Divine Prophets and Revelators in the succession of those Who had guided mankind towards the Kingdom; but their teachings apparently have been lost and are not given in the sacred text.

It is, therefore, not until the wonderful and famous prophecy of Moses in *Deuteronomy* 30 that the real story of the coming of the Kingdom of God to earth begins in the Bible.

A prophecy in the full sense of the word means much more than any mere prediction. It refers to a foreview of the future seen by an inspired Prophet by the light of eternity and is a vision of the future purpose of God laid up beyond mortal ken.

Abraham had already been told of the coming of one of His descendants in whom all the families of the earth would be blessed and Jacob similarly had foretold (*Gen.* 49) the coming of Shiloh. Moses' prophecy was more full and more exact. He foretold that, in the distant future, the

Israelites whom He was now leading from Egypt towards the Promised Land would, for a dreadful crime, be plucked out of that land, and be utterly dispersed among the nations. They would live in misery and humiliation until, in the fullness of time, the Lord God, moved with compassion, would "*return and gather*" the Israelites and restore them as His converted subjects, to the ancient land of their fathers, there to live in lasting peace.

> "*And it shall come to pass, when all these things are come upon thee, the blessing and the curse, which I have set before thee, and thou shalt call them to mind among all the nations whither the Lord thy God hath driven thee,*
>
> "*And shalt return unto the Lord thy God, and shalt obey his voice, according to all that I command thee this day, thou and thy children, with all thine heart, and with all thy soul;*
>
> "*That then the Lord thy God will turn thy captivity, and have compassion upon thee, and will return and gather thee from all the nations, whither the Lord thy God hath scattered thee.*"   (*Deut.* 30)

Moses' prediction provided the Jewish Prophets with one of their favourite and most famous themes. It was the chief subject of the greatest of them all, Isaiah, of which he wrote in his most exalted and powerful manner. Jeremiah and Ezekiel, Zechariah, Joel, Micah, Nahum, Habbakuk, Zephaniah shared his enthusiasm and filled out the enraptured picture which he gave of the future restoration. Moses' prophecy of the return became synchronized with the final coming of the Kingdom of God through the appearance of the Supreme World Redeemer, the Lord God, the Lord of Hosts. The world was to be unified and the Jews in the Holy Land were to hold a central place which would give to them a position of honour and make them the envy of mankind. The world in that day would be, as the Prophets saw it, transformed inwardly and outwardly; human character would be changed and uplifted.

> "I will give them one heart, and I will put a new spirit within you . . . that they may walk in my statutes . . . and they shall be my people, and I will be their God." *(Ezekiel* xi 19–20)

> "I will pour out my Spirit upon all flesh . . ." *(Joel* ii 28)

> "I will put my law in their inward parts, and write it in their hearts; and will be their God, and they shall be my people." *(Jeremiah* xxxi 33)

> " . . . the earth shall be full of the knowledge of the Lord, as the waters cover the sea." *(Isaiah* xi 9 and *Hab.* ii 14)

> "And the Lord shall be King over all the earth: in that day shall there be one Lord, and His Name one." *(Zech.* xiv 9)

Peace will reign everywhere through the earth. Men shall learn war no more. Security, tranquillity of mind and

THE KINGDOM IN THE BIBLE

plenty will follow peace. (*Isaiah* ii 4; *Micah* iv 4–5; *Isaiah* xxxv 1–2; *Joel* iii 18).

> "He shall judge among many people, and rebuke strong nations afar off, and they shall beat their swords into plowshares, and their spears into pruning-hooks; . . ." (*Micah* iv 3)

> "Righteousness and peace have kissed each other" adds the psalmist. (*Psalm* lxxxv 10)

The character of men shall be recognised for what it truly is:

> "The vile person shall be no more called liberal, nor the churl said to be bountiful." (*Isaiah* xxxii 5)

In the midst of this community of peaceful and friendly nations the Prophets placed the Holy Land in a position of privilege pre-eminent. In legislation, in religious instruction and in the execution of government and of justice she stands unique.

> ". . . out of Zion shall go forth the law, and the word of the Lord from Jerusalem." (*Isaiah* ii 3)

And again

> ". . . Come ye, and let us go up to the mountain of the Lord, to the house of the God of Jacob; and he will teach us of his ways, and we will walk in his paths . . . and he shall judge among the nations, and shall rebuke many people . . ." (*Isaiah* ii 3–4)

> ". . . and the government shall be upon his shoulder; and his name shall be called Wonderful, Counsellor,

The mighty God, The everlasting Father, The Prince of Peace.

"Of the increase of his government and peace there shall be no end, upon the throne of David, and upon his kingdom, to order it, and to establish it with judgment and with justice from henceforth even for ever. The zeal of the Lord of hosts will perform this."   (*Isaiah* ix 6–7)[1]

Little wonder indeed that the Jewish people from the time of Isaiah till the present hour should find solace and pride in the thought of the restoration of their people at the time of the coming of the Kingdom, and should read and re-read with happiness the prophecies of the coming of the Lord of Hosts.

Another great picture of the glory of the Kingdom is given in the Bible in the Revelation of St. John the Divine, bringing the Bible to its climax and its end. Belonging to the Revelation of Christ this naturally is of a highly spiritual order. It promises the presence of God as actually present in the Kingdom and dwelling among men.

"Behold, the tabernacle of God is with men, and he will dwell with them, and they shall be his people and God himself shall be with them, and be their God. And God shall wipe away all tears from their eyes; and there shall be no more death, neither sorrow, nor crying, neither shall there be any more pain: for the former things are passed away. . . . And they shall see his face; and his name shall be in their foreheads. And there shall be no night there; and they need no

[1] see page 27-8.

candle, neither light of the sun; for the Lord God giveth them light; and they shall reign for ever and ever." *(Revelation* xxi 3–4, xxii 4–5)

Since it is written (*Rev.* xxi 24)

"And the nations of them which are saved shall walk in the light of it: and the kings of the earth do bring their glory and honour into it",

one must infer that the reference to God's presence alludes to the earthly Kingdom and the Holy Land.

CHAPTER THREE

JESUS CHRIST, HERALD OF THE KINGDOM

MOSES had announced, and great Prophets had described in inspired language, the establishment of the Kingdom and the restoration of the Jews. Jesus' function was more intimate, more constructive, more creative. He was actually the Herald of the Kingdom, which, He said, was "at hand". But He did not reveal it fully; "*I have yet many things to say unto you, but ye cannot bear them now.*" The Kingdom, in His Revelation, becomes a living, glowing reality, both within the believer's heart and shortly to be fulfilled in the world. Jesus reveals its King as none had done before Him, and testifies of Him as "*he shall testify of me*".

Jesus created a power of perceiving God which was new, and in order that it might operate clearly, had to cleanse the spirit of man from all worldly encumbrances. Virtue became detachment from the world, sin attachment to it. Jesus demanded this sacrifice—losing the life of the world for the life of the spirit, but He made God so attractive, so joyous, loving, powerful, that the Christian was ready to abandon all for Him, and for Christ Who revealed Him.

Thus the tremendous and fearsome Deity of the Old Testament wins men's hearts in the New. We read of the poor sparrow whose fall was watched by a loving Father, of the flower of the field and the bird of the air, and the tenderest stories that ever have won men's hearts—the prodigal son and the good Samaritan.

A new quality of love now characterizes the Kingdom, a love which united the believers not only with God, but with each other, and even extended to enemies and *"them that hate you." "That ye love one another"* became the test of Christian discipleship.

The supreme ideal of this love was, as shown in *John*, the relationship between Christ and the Father, and though revealed in the most simple language and the plainest words, stands as the highest expression of Divine love in scripture.

The result was that Jesus' teachings let loose upon the soul and heart of man a spiritual power such as never had been known in the world before. Historians have said that Jesus' teaching has done more to elevate human nature and civilization than all the laws of legislators and the disquisitions of philosophers combined. By releasing religious energies measured to the needs of the hour and the people, He opened the way to the Kingdom of God in men's hearts. New affections and aspirations, hopes and loyalties were brought into being and the whole moral world was carried into a state of flux.

The early Christians taught the sacredness of human life and the dignity of human nature. As soon as they could they stopped the exposure of infants at birth and the practice of gladiatorial shows. Later they promoted education, built hospitals and introduced a juster system of legislation than had been in use in the Roman State before. Such changes as these they made because the seat of Christ's government was fixed in their souls and His throne was in their hearts. They lay open to the impress

B

of every breath the Spirit breathed on them and had consecrated their wills to His service. A new and Christian civilization arose, centred on Byzantium, which reached its height in the fourth century.[1]

In Jesus' time there was a great company of brilliant philosophers, historians and orators, poets and scholars in Rome, all of them deeply conscious of the debasement and the disintegration of Roman life, particularly anxious to find a way of improving it and all truly unable to do so. The thought that the new teaching of Christ would prove equal to the task and would rebuild a new and better social order never occurred to one of them. They seldom mentioned Christianity and when they did, referred to it in terms of complete contempt. Men have marvelled at their blindness, but after all the cause is not far to seek: Jesus regards this human world as antagonistic to the divine world. "*Ye cannot serve God and mammon*" is the cornerstone of His ethics. Unless a man hates his father and his mother, his wife and his home for His sake and the Gospel's he cannot be His disciple. He demands, therefore, that a man shall exercise a high degree of self-control and self-discipline. Jesus taught that this earth life is intended to be a bridge to pass over and not a home in which to take up one's abode. The wise man, therefore, who passes this way will not attach himself to too many ties but will keep himself free so that he will be able, if some higher call of duty comes to him from the divine world, to follow it at once. He will seek to achieve a high standard of self-control and self-discipline, happily conscious that the demands of the Gospel and of Christ take precedence over any earthly imperative.

[1] See Chap. 9.

The Roman philosopher, on the other hand, immersed completely in the affairs, interests and calls of the human world, has no conception whatever of any obligation to sacrifice its need to those of a higher existence.

Purity, therefore, is the cleansing of the human heart from the obscuring influence of the mists and shadows of earth which do not enable man to see any vision of God or of Christ but keep him in comparative darkness, knowing nothing of the vision or the power which comes to the heart that has disengaged itself from all love of Mammon. The wonders of Christ could never have come to pass, nor could the spiritual energies, shed so bountifully, have been released had He not been ready to sacrifice every human tie and attachment for the sake of God and God's beloved. The mysterious power which comes of sacrifice like Christ's, and in no other way, is similar to that of a seed which falls into the ground and is buried in the dark. The seed gives up its outer life and the shell perishes; instead the inner being of the seed takes on a new life of its own which spreads and expands into a very big tree, assuming a new form in the boughs and branches and leaves. Analogously, Christ abandoned all that held Him to home and all the ties of earth, and this sacrifice created the Christian community into which His own life passed. He was the first to make the sacrifice His teachings demanded and God-intoxicated apostles, following Him, went forth to transform the world and die as martyrs.

Bahá'u'lláh testifies:—

"... that when the Son of Man yielded up His breath to God, the whole creation wept with a great weeping. By sacrificing Himself, however, a fresh capacity was infused into all created things. Its evidences, as witnessed in all the peoples of the earth, are now manifest before thee. The deepest wisdom which the sages have uttered, the profoundest learning which any mind hath unfolded, the arts which the ablest hands have produced, the influence exerted by the most potent of rulers, are but manifestations of the quickening power released by His transcendent, His all-pervasive, and resplendent Spirit.

"We testify that when He came into the world, He shed the splendour of His glory upon all created things. Through Him the leper recovered from the leprosy of perversity and ignorance. Through Him, the unchaste and wayward were healed. Through His power, born of Almighty God, the eyes of the blind were opened, and the soul of the sinner sanctified.

"Leprosy may be interpreted as any veil that interveneth between man and the recognition of the Lord, his God. Whoso alloweth himself to be shut out from Him is indeed a leper, who shall not be remembered in the Kingdom of God, the Mighty, the All-Praised. We bear witness that through the power of the Word of God every leper was cleansed, every sickness was healed, every human infirmity was banished. He it is Who purified the world. Blessed is the man who, with a face beaming with light, hath turned towards Him."[1]

Wonderful is the story of Christ indeed! Yet where is the Gospel in the world to-day?

[1] *Gleanings from the Writings of Bahá'u'lláh*, section xxxvi.

CHAPTER FOUR

THE FALSE PROPHETS

As Jesus had prophesied, the false prophets contrived to change the essential meaning of the Gospel so that it became quite different from that which the Bible recorded or Jesus taught.[1]

It has long been generally believed that Jesus Christ was a unique incarnation of God such as had never before appeared in religious history and would never appear again. This tenet made the acceptance of any later Prophet impossible to a Christian. Yet there is nothing in Christ's own statements, as recorded in the Gospel, to support this view, and it was not generally held during His lifetime.

Jesus emphatically claimed to reveal God, Whom He called Father, but continually differentiated Himself from the Father. In many such references as *"Him that sent me,"* *"my Father is greater than I,"*[2] *"I go to the Father,"*[3] *"I will pray the Father,"*[4] *"I do nothing of myself; but as my Father hath taught me,"*[5] He made this abundantly clear, and even stated specifically that the Father had knowledge which was not possessed by the Son. *"But of that day and that hour knoweth no man, no, not the angels which are in heaven,*

[1] *Matt.* vii 15–23 and see pp. 11, 12.
[2] *John* xiv 28.
[3] *John* xvi 16.
[4] *John* xiv 16.
[5] *John* viii 28.

neither the Son, but the Father."[1] He referred to Himself as
the Son, and as a Prophet,[2] and was so regarded,[3] and
related His Mission to those of Moses and Abraham before
Him, and to others to come after Him, specifically "*he,
the Spirit of truth,*" who would reveal the things which
Jesus did not.[4]

The followers of every world religion have invented
for themselves a similar belief in the uniqueness and
finality of their own Prophet. The result has been that
no religion has acknowledged a Prophet of a later
religion. The Hindus do not acknowledge Buddha, the
Buddhists do not acknowledge Christ, nor yet do the
Zoroastrians. The result of this delusive belief has been
that the world religions have not tended to the unifying
of mankind but rather to its further division.

Another opinion which Christians universally hold
about Christ is that His teaching was absolute and final.
They believe that if the Truth were partly withheld from
them for a time because they could not bear it, it was
divulged at Pentecost in its fullness and that now nothing
remains to be revealed. But there is nothing in the account
of Pentecost to suggest such an interpretation and there
is no one who will believe that Jesus would have named
the false prophets as characteristic of His age if this
warning was to be followed by an immediate release of all
Truth to the Church. What the Bible shows is rather a
succession of teachers—Abraham, Moses and Christ, each
measuring His Revelation to the needs and maturity of
His auditors: Jesus, for example, changes the divorce law

[1] *Mark* xiii 32.
[2] *Matt.* xiii 57, *Luke* xiii 33.
[3] *Matt.* xxi 11, *Luke* vii 16.
[4] *John* xvi 12, 13.

and says, "*Moses gave you this because of the hardness of your hearts but from the beginning it was not so.*" Many times He says, "*Ye have heard it said by them of old time . . . but I say unto you . . .*"

Another universal opinion among the Christians is that Christ was the Lord of Hosts of the old Testament. Yet the Jewish Prophets had foretold that when the Lord of Hosts came He would not find the Jews in the Holy Land, all would have been scattered among the nations and would have been living in misery and degradation for centuries; but when Jesus came Palestine was full of Jews and their expulsion did not begin until the year 70 A.D.; it may be said to have continued till the year 1844.

To confirm orthodox Christian opinion it is customary in all churches to read on Christmas morning, as if it referred to Jesus, the passage which Isaiah wrote about the Lord of Hosts (*Isaiah* ix 6-7).

> "For unto us a child is born, unto us a son is given: and the government shall be upon his shoulder: and his name shall be called Wonderful, Counsellor, The mighty God, The everlasting Father, The Prince of Peace. Of the increase of his government and peace there shall be no end, upon the throne of David, and upon his kingdom, to order it, and to establish it with judgment and with justice from henceforth even for ever. The zeal of the Lord of hosts will perform this."

Yet the descriptive titles given do not belong exclusively to Christ, while some of them He specifically repudiated as if to make such a mistaken reference to Himself impossible. He disclaimed being the Mighty God when He called Himself *"the Son of God;"*[1] disclaimed being the Father when He said, *"my Father is greater than I;"*[2] and being the Prince of Peace when He said, *"I came not to send peace, but a sword."*[3] He disclaimed bearing the government upon His shoulder or that it would be His judgment and justice forever when He said, *"My kingdom is not of this world."*[4]

Many of these false interpretations involve repudiation of the Word of God in favour of the word of man. This impious act is so craftily performed, with such an air of humility, that it might escape the notice of the most sincere and devout of worshippers. Probably few church-goers realize to-day that the Gospel of Christ as known to the few in the pulpit is wholly different from the Gospel which Christ preached in Galilee as recorded in the Bible.

In spite of Christ's promise of further revelation of Truth, through the Comforter, through His own return, through the Spirit of Truth, the Christian Church regards His revelation as final, and itself as the sole trustee of true religion. There is no room for the Supreme Redeemer of the Bible to bring in great changes for the establishment of the Kingdom of God. In fact this Kingdom is often described as a world-wide Church.

Having thus closed God's Covenant with the Bible, sacred history—God-directed—came to an end, and secular history, having no sense of divine destiny nor unity, began.

[1] *John* v 18–47 where Jesus repudiates the charge that He claimed equality with God.
[2] *John* xiv 28.
[3] *Matt.* x 34.
[4] *John* xviii 36.

Jesus' revelation was purely spiritual. He taught that "*My kingdom is not of this world*" and that the "*kingdom of heaven is within you.*" His great gift to man was the knowledge of eternal life. He told men that they might be physically in perfect health and yet spiritually sick or even dead. But this was a difficult truth to communicate and Jesus had to help men to realize it. He would say that He was a spiritual physician and that men whom He cured of a spiritual disability were cured of blindness, deafness, lameness, leprosy and so on. This was the real meaning of His remark at the end of a discourse, "*He that hath ears to hear, let him hear.*" For a hearer might hear the physical word of Jesus and yet fail to comprehend the spiritual meaning. Jesus, in other words, was forever trying to heal spiritual infirmities. He thus would be understood by His disciples as a healer of spiritual ailments but by others He might be taken as relieving physical ills only.

Doubtless Jesus could, and often did, heal bodily ills by spiritual means, but this was nothing to do with His real work as a Redeemer. On the other hand these spiritual cures which He effected might be misinterpreted as physical miracles, and so were little stressed by Him. ("*See that no man know it.*"[1])

Christ's spiritual mission was, at an early date, materialized, specifically in regard to such things as the miracles, curing the blind and deaf, raising the dead. Even His own resurrection was made physical, missing the point entirely. Moreover, none of the complex order, of the ceremonies, rituals and litanies of the Church can be attributed to Christ. All are man-made, by inference or invention.

[1] *Matt.* ix 30.

Well might Christ warn His followers that false prophets would arise and misinterpret His teachings so as to delude even the most earnest and intelligent of His believers: from early times Christians have disputed about Christian truth in councils, in sects, in wars.

To sum up, if Christians say "our acts may be wrong," they say truly. If they say "however our Gospel is right" they are quite wrong. The false prophets have corrupted the Gospel as successfully as they have the deeds and lives of Christian people.

CHAPTER FIVE

MUḤAMMAD, BUILDER OF NATIONS

IT might seem natural to expect that the Dispensation of the Herald of the Kingdom would be followed in sequence by that of the King whose Herald He was. But this was not to be. It had been already so announced in the Book of Genesis.

God foretold to Abraham that the Prophetic succession was to run through Him and be fulfilled not only in Isaac but in Ishmael. In *Genesis* xii 1–2 it is written "Now the Lord had said unto Abram, . . . I will make of thee a great nation, and I will bless thee, and make thy name great; and thou shalt be a blessing:" And again in *Genesis* xvii 20 "And as for Ishmael, I have heard thee: Behold I have blessed him, . . . and will multiply him exceedingly; twelve princes shall he beget, and I will make him a great nation." The narrative continues (*Gen.* xxi 20–21) "God was with the lad; and he grew, . . . and he dwelt in the wilderness of Paran: and . . . took him a wife out of the land of Egypt."

He became the progenitor of the people of Arabia and the twelve Princes which he begot are interpreted as the twelve Imams who followed Muḥammad.

Moses confirmed this promise when He prophesied (*Deut.* xviii 15) to the Israelites that *"the Lord thy God will raise up unto thee a Prophet from the midst of thee, of thy brethren, like unto me."* This refers not only to the coming of Jesus Christ, as is usually thought, but more especially to Muḥammad. Moses would have used the word "seed" if He had meant to refer to an Israelite, whereas the word "brethren" indicates that He alludes to Isaac's brother Ishmael. He connects Mount Paran explicitly with the Prophetic line when, in His final blessing before His death, He describes the Prophets who will follow Him: "*The Lord came from Sinai* (meaning Himself), *and rose up from Seir* . . . (meaning Jesus Christ); *he shined forth from mount Paran* (meaning Muḥammad), *and he came with ten thousands of saints* (meaning Baha'u'-llah)." *Deut. xxxiii 2.*

On the other hand Muḥammad mentions in the Qur'án the prophecies of His coming made in the Bible (Sura 26 verses 192–199) and states that Abraham prayed for His coming (Sura 2 verses 118–144) and that He was foretold by Moses and described in the Law and the Evangel.

Mankind had now had the experience of organizing the family, the tribe and the city state. Before humanity could proceed to the task of organizing the far superior government of the Commonwealth of Baha'u'llah a preliminary lesson in the art of building a nation had to be given. This constituted, as the Guardian of the Bahá'í Faith shows on pages 124-5 of *The Promised Day is Come*, the special mission of the Arabian Prophet whose advent Moses had foretold. "*Of old it hath been revealed: 'Love of one's country is an element of the Faith of God'*" said Baha'u'lláh with reference to this appointed task.

The conditions of Muḥammad's life were not such as to make this mission easy. Born in Mecca, the capital city of Arabia, about 570, He found Himself in the midst of a people consisting of a hundred warlike tribes, inheriting a tradition of polytheism, who had resisted all efforts at evangelization and who regarded battle as the only occupation fit for men. Such was the race whom Muḥammad was to convert to monotheism and to unify into an unbreakable band of brothers, their unity being based on their religious faith.

Muḥammad was already about forty years old when He began to teach ethical principles similar to those of the Old Testament and to proclaim the succession of the Prophets, including His own succession to Jesus Christ, Whose divinity and Whose Gospel he called His believers to accept. But after a few years He found Himself forced by severe and continuous persecution to leave His native town for Medina where He at once began the execution of the real mission of His life, the building of a spiritual nation.

Western scholars seem to be at one in regarding nationalism as Muḥammad's real and creative contribution to human development. They all have recognized the extraordinary ability displayed by Him in organizing and consolidating the wild tribes of Arabia. Sir William Muir for instance wrote that ". . . he, with consummate skill, devised a machinery, by the adaptive energy of which he gradually shaped the broken and disconnected masses of the Arab race into an harmonious whole, a body politic endowed with life and vigour . . . by unparalleled art and a rare supremacy of mind, he persuaded the whole of Arabia, Pagan, Jew, and Christian, to follow his steps with docile submission." (*The Life of Mahomet* p. lxxxvi).[1]

T. W. Arnold in *The Preaching of Islám*[2] writes in the

---

[1] Smith, Elder & Co., London, 3rd ed. 1894.
[2] Constable, London, 2nd ed. 1913.

same vein. "The Arab tribes were thus impelled to give in their submission to the Prophet, not merely as the head of the strongest military force in Arabia, but as the exponent of a theory of social life that was making all others weak and ineffective. Muḥammad had succeeded in introducing into the anarchical society of his time a sentiment of national unity, a consciousness of rights and duties towards one another such as the Arabs had not felt before" (pp. 40-41).

The outstanding features which distinguish Muḥammad's system may be summarized under nine points:

1. Patriotism was a part of the Faith.
2. Only Muslims were full citizens; minorities, such as Christians and Jews, enjoyed freedom and protection, but not the full brotherhood of Islám.
3. There was one compulsory language for all, the adoption of which was made a basic condition for citizenship in the Muḥammadan empire.
4. There was no class distinction, and an equality of rights among all Muslims was established.
5. There was unity in ritual and religious tradition.
6. There was freedom of thought and reconciliation of science and religion.
7. There was a juridical system with its laws and courts of justice independent of the will of the Government.
8. True and real membership in the nation was assured to every citizen as in a modern democracy.
9. It was a theocratic state.

An original combination of the two contrasted but complementary theories of theocracy and democracy seems to be the strong base of Muḥammad's system and Professor de Santillana in his essay[1] in *The Legacy of Islám* explains clearly how this combination was effected. He shows that Muḥammad swept away the former limited loyalties of tribe and family. A believer who adopted Islám must forget and forego his own kith and kin unless they were his companions in the Faith. All connections pended on religion alone. The community of Islám was different from any other. It was the chosen of God to whom was entrusted the furtherance of good and the repression of evil. It was the sole witness for God among the nations, the sole seat of justice and faith in the world. Instead of the impersonal life of the tribe there emerged the personal life of the individual which took its claims and its duties not from membership of the community but from adherence to the Faith. Patriotism was thus the element of faith.

"Islam is the direct government of Alláh, the rule of God . . . upon his people. . . . Alláh is the name of the supreme power, acting in the common interest . . . between Alláh and the believer there is no mediator; Islam has no church, no priests, no sacraments . . . Man is alone in the presence of God, in life and in death . . . to Whom is present every action, every word . . .; alone he will answer for his deeds, and alone will he face the judgement of God . . . The most rigid protestantism is almost a sacerdotal religion, compared with this personal mono-theism, unbending, and intolerant of any interference between man and his Creator"[1] (pp. 286-287).

Quoting the Islámic principle that the "object of

[1] *Law and Society; The Legacy of Islam,* ed. Sir Thomas Arnold
and A. Guillaume. O.U.P. 1931.

Government is to lead men to prosperity in this world
and to salvation in the next," the Professor writes that
" *'the white man is not above the black nor the black above
the yellow; all men are equal before their Maker'*, said the
Prophet. Equal before God, members of a great family in
which there is neither noble nor villein, but only believers,
Muslims are equal before the civil law; and this equality
was proclaimed at a time when it was practically unknown
throughout Christian society. This law, equal for all,
rests essentially on *good faith*. Muslims must keep their
pledges . . . This conception of good faith is essentially an
ethical one, and is elevated to an abstract and universal
notion. It strikes us as being more akin to our mind
than the feudal and Germanic conception of good faith
springing from personal fealty" (p. 304).

It was evidently the intention of Muḥammad to make
Islám not only a model organization but a model in its
international relations. The Prophet insisted that the
Muslim state was to observe its treaties as sacred. "*Ye who
believe*" He writes in the Qur'án, "*be not false in your
engagements, with your own knowledge. . . . Or if thou fear
treachery from any people, throw back their treaty to them as
thou fairly mayest, for God loveth not the treacherous. . . . And
if they lean to peace, lean thou also to it.*" (Sura 8 verses
27, 60, 63). He warns his followers that if they make a
treaty with infidels and the infidels remain true to it
they too must keep their engagements "*with them through the
whole time of their treaty; for God loveth those who fear Him.
. . . But if, after alliance made, they break their oaths and revile
your religion, then do battle with the ring-leaders of infidelity—
for no oaths are binding with them—that they may desist.*"
(Sura 9 verses 4 and 12). Muḥammad Himself strictly

observed the principles of justice in His public as in His private dealings. The wars which He waged were not like those of earthly conquerors undertaken for spoliation or aggrandizement, but were called for by the lawless conditions of the time. They were intended to protect the Faith and its followers and were not pursued further than was necessary for this protective purpose.

The originality of such practical regulations and the need for introducing and enforcing them in the anarchical international life of those days may be judged from the following excerpt from *The Spirit of Islám*, page 209:[1]

"The Romans . . . could never realise the duties of international morality or of humanity. They waged war for the sole purpose of subjugating the surrounding nations. . . . The sacredness of treaties was unknown. . . . The liberty of other nations was never of the slightest importance in their estimation. The introduction of Christianity made little or no change in the views entertained by its professors concerning international obligations. War was as inhuman and as exterminating as before. . . . Christianity did not profess to deal with international morality, and so left its followers groping in the dark."

According to a tradition which is probably true and which in the case of the Persian king is endorsed by Bahá'u'lláh Himself, Muḥammad sent from Medina letters of friendship, proclaiming His Prophethood, to six neighbouring rulers: to the Emperor of Byzantium, the Emperor of Persia, the King of Abyssinia, the Governor of Egypt, the King of Hira, the Duke of Yemen in Central Arabia—and also to the Emperor of China (in 628 A.D.) which was then under the T'ang dynasty and

[1] Syed Ameer 'Alí, *The Spirit of Islám*, Christophers, London, Rev. 1922.

entering a golden age. Thus did He seek kindly relationships between Himself and the rulers of other peoples and
took a bold initiative in setting internationalism on a
sound basis of law and justice.

"*Let there be in you a nation summoning unto the good*" is
a divine order in the Qur'án. And in spite of dissensions
and civil wars, some length of time elapsed before the
Muslim conscience countenanced any such division of
nationalities as we have seen to be characteristic of the
Islám of our time; and the spread of one language over the
whole of the conquered territory was carried with far
greater success and determination than the Romans ever
achieved or displayed. For at one time the Arabic language
dominated the whole Islámic area from Spain and North
Africa to Central Asia; it tolerated no rival language as
Latin tolerated Greek.

Syed Ameer 'Alí sums up the contribution of Islám
to political science in the following remarkable comment:

"Islám gave to the people a code which, however
archaic in its simplicity, was capable of the greatest
development in accordance with the progress of material
civilisation. It conferred on the State a flexible constitution, based on a just appreciation of human rights and
human duty. It limited taxation, it made men equal in the
eye of the law, it consecrated the principles of self-govern-
ment. It established a control over the sovereign power
by rendering the executive authority subordinate to the
law—a law based upon religious sanction and moral
obligations. 'The excellence and effectiveness of each of
these principles', says Urquhart, '(each capable of immor-
talising its founder), gave value to the rest; and all combined, endowed the system which they formed with a

force and energy exceeding those of any other political system. Within the lifetime of a man, though in the hands of a population wild, ignorant, and insignificant, it spread over a greater extent than the dominions of Rome. While it retained its primitive character, it was irresistible.' "[1]

[1] Urquhart, *The Spirit of the East*, vol. i, intro. xxviii.
   Syed Ameer 'Alí, *The Spirit of Islám*, p. 277.

CHAPTER SIX

MUḤAMMAD AND THE CHRISTIANS

To the Christians Muḥammad showed the greatest kindness. Insisting that all Muslims should fully accept both Jesus Christ and His Gospel, and assuring them in the Qur'án (Sura 5 verse 85) that they would find the Christians nearest of all men to them in affection, He took the Christians under his express protection.

A remarkable illustration of this is afforded by the charter which Muḥammad granted to the Christians in general and to the monks of the monastery of St. Catherine, near Mount Sinai, in particular, the actual document itself having been faithfully preserved down the centuries by the analysts of Islám.

Quoting this charter in *The Spirit of Islám* (p. 84) Syed Ameer 'Alí remarks that it "has been justly designated as one of the noblest monuments of enlightened tolerance that the history of the world can produce," and he calls attention to its marvellous breadth of view and liberality of conception.[1] "By it," he writes, "the Prophet secured to the Christians privileges and immunities which they did not possess even under sovereigns of their own creed; and declared that any Moslem violating and abusing what

[1] That this charter represented the firm attitude of tolerance and goodwill which the Prophet was accustomed to show towards Christians may be judged from the terms of a parallel charter to the Christians of Najrán which is quoted by the author in the same work on page 273.

was therein ordered, should be regarded as a violator of God's testament, a transgressor of His commandments, and a slighter of His Faith. He undertook himself, and enjoined on his followers, to protect the Christians, to defend their churches, the residences of their priests, and to guard them from all injuries. They were not to be unfairly taxed; no bishop was to be driven out of his bishopric; no Christian was to be forced to reject his religion; no monk was to be expelled from his monastery; no pilgrim was to be detained from his pilgrimage. Nor were the Christian churches to be pulled down for the sake of building mosques or houses for the Moslems. Christian women married to Moslems were to enjoy their own religion, and not to be subjected to compulsion or annoyance of any kind on that account. If Christians should stand in need of assistance for the repair of their churches or monasteries, or any other matter pertaining to their religion, the Moslems were to assist them. This was not to be considered as taking part in their religion, but as merely rendering them assistance in their need, and complying with the ordinances of the Prophet which were made in their favour by the authority of God and of His Apostle. Should the Moslems be engaged in hostilities with outside Christians, no Christian resident among the Moslems should be treated with contempt on account of his creed. Any Moslem so treating a Christian should be accounted recalcitrant to the Prophet."

No Christian student reading Muhammad's teachings can miss the fact that His ethical system corrected many of those corruptions which had crept into the Christian Faith of the seventh century. For instance Muhammad preached an emphatic monotheism in place of a trinitarian

Godhead. He left no room for that sacerdotalism which had so enervated and distorted the spirit of the Gospel. He encouraged and promoted in the strongest way the pursuit of science and learning which had become anathema to Christian orthodoxy; He is believed to have said that the ink of the scholar was more holy than the blood of the martyr and to have bidden believers to go as far as China for knowledge if necessary. Instead of endorsing celibacy He honoured marriage, home life and home duties and by the stress He laid on the oneness of all believers and the paramount duty of brotherly loyalty He showed His horror of schism.

So kindly were the relations between the two Faiths and so strong the spiritual influence of Muḥammad that the Christian masses were disposed to accept the Faith of the Arabian Prophet. The Báb indeed says that they were only prevented from doing so by the failure of the clergy *"for if these had believed, they would have been followed by the mass of their countrymen."* Had it not been for the unfortunate divisive counsel of these Christian priests, history would have been different indeed.

CHAPTER SEVEN

THE VIOLATION OF
MUḤAMMAD'S COVENANT

Muḥammad completed His mission. Out of the unpromising material presented to Him He had created a spiritual nation such as the world had never seen and one which would prove itself possessed of a solidarity and effectiveness which have always been the wonder of mankind. The future would depend on the loyalty, the understanding and sympathy of His followers and on the guidance given them by their leaders.

Moses had appointed Joshua as His immediate successor and as long as Joshua led the Israelites the sun of Moses shone high in the heavens. Jesus appointed Peter to succeed Him, without notifying him as to the limit of his authority or who was to succeed him in his office, if anyone. Muḥammad, without naming him, designated ʿAlí, His son-in-law, by signs so many and so striking that no one could mistake their meaning and, what is more, Muḥammad had with him a number of conversations dealing with the future of the Cause and the nature of its development. Muḥammad also stated in plain terms that His family and His book were to succeed Him, thus in effect giving to ʿAlí, as His son-in-law, the right of succession to the place of the Prophet.

But sectional loyalties, tribal jealousies and personal ambition all conspired to defeat Muḥammad's purpose. ʿAlí, whose character and outstanding ability made him conspicuously suited for the position to which Muḥammad had appointed him, was set aside,[1] and Islám was thus deprived, until too late, of the inspired guidance which he could have given it. Because of this violation of the Covenant, the spirit and meaning of the Islámic Faith were degraded, weakened and poisoned. Faction grew, the Prophet's family was dispossessed, and before long the powerful Umayyad clan, which had opposed Muḥammad more bitterly than any other, gained the ascendancy, to rule Islám as an Arab empire with little regard for religion or the precepts of the Prophet.

'Abdu'l-Bahá describes this clan as the beast from the bottomless pit that warred against the spiritual life of Islám and killed it, leaving nothing of the religion of Muḥammad but the prayers and the fast; all the justice, the righteousness, the mercy and indeed all the virtues which the Prophet had enshrined in Islám were irretrievably lost.

Deprived of the guidance of Muḥammad's family and ruled by descendants of Muḥammad's enemies, Islám was transformed into a secular state whose rulers used religion for secular ends. Muḥammad's plans remained unknown and so remain to this day, though it is easy to surmise their general character.

This heinous violation swept away all possibility of Muḥammad's love for Christendom, so conspicuously displayed in His lifetime, from developing, and thereafter the relationship of these two chief civilizations followed its tragic course, continuing right down to our own day to disturb the order of the world and to prevent the establishment of that unity in brotherhood which was the desire of both Christ and Muḥammad.

[1] They said he was too young.

CHAPTER EIGHT

CHRISTIANITY AND ISLÁM

I SLÁM, having lost a great part of its spiritual power and having to divert its manifold energies chiefly to secular ends, went forward on its conquering career, driving the Christians out of Palestine, out of North Africa, out of most of Spain, but being stopped in France by the battle of Tours. Western Christendom on the other hand sank back into the Dark Ages and languished in semi-barbarism for centuries.

'Umar and the Caliphs who followed him rapidly extended the Muslim empire from the Pillars of Hercules to Calicut. In the midst of a dark and stagnant world there sprang up as if by magic a brilliant civilization. In 760 A.D. its rulers moved their capital from Damascus to Baghdád and founded on the site of an ancient Christian village a city which became at once a world centre of culture and commerce, and so remained for five centuries. All phases of civilization as then known were there found gathered together and renewed, and in many cases carried to heights never reached before: letters and language, the arts, the sciences, both practical and abstract, trade, transport and seamanship, invention and industry, jurisprudence and the arts of government. Because of the central position of the Qur'án, revered as a literary miracle, and because of Arabian pride in their language, which they held to be the one perfect tongue spoken by man and which is indeed regarded by scholars to-day as one of the greatest intellectual achievements of the race, literature in all its uses and forms was given a place of eminence. Schools and universities were founded and thronged by students of many nations. Great works were produced on all manner of subjects; great libraries were collected containing hundreds of thousands of volumes. The Caliphs ransacked the earth for knowledge, sending out expeditions of inquiry and making foreign lands and distant ages give up their lore. An army of translators was employed, rendering Greek, Egyptian, Indian and Jewish works into Arabic. Grammar and its laws were studied with great elaboration. Dictionaries, lexicons and encyclopaedias on a vast scale were prepared. Paper was introduced from China; a new system of numerals (usually known as Arabic) from India. Arabic became the universal language. Caliphs would invite literary men of international repute to the court. Scholars, philosophers, poets, grammarians from diverse lands would find a meeting place in the great bookshops of the capital.

The pursuit of science, practical as well as abstract, kept pace with that of letters. In experimental science, in medicine and surgery, in chemistry and physics, in geography as well as in mathematics and astronomy, the Arabs led the world of that day. They invented a new and exquisite form of architecture, distinguished by its combination of airy grace with solid strength, and by its use of light. The influence of this style can be traced through India as far as Java, to China, to the Sudan and to the whole of Russia. They developed many branches of industry and improved methods of agriculture and horticulture. Introducing the use of the mariner's compass their ships traversed the seas while caravans maintained a trade between all provinces of the empire, carrying produce from India and China, Turkistan and Russia, from Africa and the Malayan Archipelago.

The glory of Baghdád with its mosques and palaces, its temples of learning, its fragrant gardens, was reproduced in the lesser centres of the world of Islám: in Basra, in Bokhara, in Granada and Cordoba. It is written of the last-named city that at the height of its prosperity it contained more than 20,000 houses and more than a million inhabitants and that a man after sunset might walk in a straight line for ten miles along paved and illuminated streets—yet in Europe centuries later there was not a paved street in Paris nor a public lamp in London.

Cordoba was the first University founded in Europe, and in its halls multitudes of Christian scholars received instruction, among them being Gerbert who afterwards became Sylvester II, the brilliant Pope of Rome.

Inevitably, and in spite of the antagonism between Christendom and Islám, this advanced civilization influenced the course of life and thought in Europe. Through the Muslim outpost in Sicily and the scintillating brilliance of Muslim Spain, through the intelligence of scholars and the resources of the Muslim universities, through traders, through diplomats and travellers, through soldiers, sailors and reconquered peasants, new ideas, techniques and attitudes passed from Islám to Western Europe.

Then came the day in 1094 when the Pope called on the chivalry and the faithful of Christendom to arouse themselves and go forth and drive the Saracen hosts out of the sacred Christian shrine, which they had seized, and re-establish the Christian Faith in its ancient home. Europe leapt up at his word and for well-nigh two hundred years the vicissitudes of this colossal war between Europe and Asia, the West and the East, Christian and unbeliever continued to cause the loss of millions of lives, to spread infinite misery and to squander immense treasure. The Christians ultimately withdrew in ignominious and complete defeat and Islám remained in possession of all the Holy Places she had owned before.

It was Europe, however, and not Arabia which gained from the struggle, for the Crusades provided yet another channel through which knowledge of the Muslim civilization flowed into Europe. For two hundred years the leading men of Europe were constantly going to and fro between the two continents gaining not only a first-hand knowledge of the great culture in Syria but gaining too an immense emancipation of the human spirit.

Gradually, under this many-pronged impulse from the East, the obscurantism of the mediaeval Church in Western Europe gave way and finally, at the Renaissance, went down to defeat. The Renaissance was truly an expression of the *joie de vivre* which Europe learned from the Arabs, and from the Renaissance flowed those features of the Islámic culture with which the awakened Europeans began to build a richer, happier, more eager civilization than they had ever before dreamed of.

Christendom has been slow to realize and to admit the debt which our Western civilization owes to the East. But the facts of our borrowing are written large in history and nothing but prejudice can lead us to minimize our indebtedness.

"Let us examine the two civilizations" wrote Seignobos in his *Histoire de la Civilisation au Moyen Age,* "which, in the eleventh century divided the ancient world. In the west—miserable little cities, peasants' huts and great fortresses—a country always troubled by a war, where one could not travel ten leagues without running the risk of being robbed; and in the Orient—Constantinople, Cairo, Damascus, Baghdád—with their marble palaces, their workshops, their schools, their bazaars, their villages, and the incessant movement of merchants who travelled in peace from Spain to Persia. There is no doubt that the musselman and Byzantine worlds were richer, better policed, better lighted than the western world. In the eleventh century these two worlds began to become acquainted; the barbarous Christians came into contact with the civilized musselmans in two ways—by war and by commerce. And by contact with the orientals, the occidentals became civilized."[1]

[1] See *The Secret of Divine Civilization* by 'Abdu'l-Bahá, pp. 92-94 (Bahá'í Publishing Trust, Wilmette, Illinois, 1957). For statement of specific gains from Islám see *History of Mediaeval Civilization* by Charles Seignobos, pp. 117-118 (Unwin, London, 1908).

CHAPTER NINE

THE RISE OF MODERN EUROPE

IT is customary to call the civilization of modern Europe *par excellence* Christian and to think of it as the special trustee of Christian truth among the less enlightened peoples of the East. Yet in the twentieth century when the time of spiritual harvesting had come we find 'Abdu'l-Bahá saying that the West as well as the East had *"imagined themselves as having attained a glorious pinnacle of achievement and prosperity, when in reality they have touched the innermost depths of heedlessness and deprived themselves wholly of God's bounteous gifts."* Nor can they have imagined the awfulness of the crisis which western civilization would be called upon to face, nor the challenge and the strain to which it would be subjected.

The true Christian civilization is in fact not that of modern Europe but that of the age of Constantine, which far more perfectly mirrored the teachings of Christ and was inspired by the religious spirit of the early Church. Brief as that civilization was it is described by 'Abdu'l-Bahá as having been the best and most enlightened in the world *at that time.* Among its good deeds and pious acts it established infirmaries, hospitals and charitable institutions. Most of the believers reached a degree of moral perfection, had no fear of death, longed for wisdom and justice; were ready to forsake their personal profit, seeking instead to please God and spending their lives in educating and instructing the people. The Emperor Constantine himself was the first in the Roman Empire to found a public hospital for the treatment of poor people who had no one to care for them. He was the first Roman Emperor to throw himself heart and soul into the Cause of Christ. He resolutely promulgated the principles of the Gospel and brought justice and moderation into the methods of the Roman government which previously had been noted for injustice and oppression.

But in, and after, the Dark Ages, Christianity showed more interest in rites and doctrines than in moral conduct. Indeed it is said that since the time of St. Francis of Assisi no Christian reform movement has been concerned with reform of Christian conduct but rather with doctrines and rites. Even the Reformation itself, great, deep and enduring as its effects have been, was less concerned with the correction of morals than with the remedying of ritual abuses.

The whole process of building a new civilization in the West, found itself vigorously opposed by the Christian Church, which for centuries past had adopted a policy of immobility and objected to both the idea and practice of progress. As European culture advanced continuously this stagnant immobility became definite reaction and the whole spirit of the Church became hostile to all forward movement. Before the time of Muḥammad the Church had objected to the scientific spirit as well as to investigation and logic. Muḥammad had taught and encouraged science, learning and reason, and as the Church would not weaken its opposition it found itself more and more estranged from human progress.

The civilization of the West, resulting from the impact of Islám on Christendom proved to be one of enormous and ever-extending material power. Its dominion spread to an unexampled degree over the rest of the world in economic, political and military matters. But it proved quite unequal to spreading its spiritual influence. Even when, during the eighteenth and nineteenth centuries, it spent large sums of money and sent out hundreds and even thousands of missionaries, its failure to Christianize the world was as conspicuous as its success in establishing its economic suzerainty. Viewing the whole period from the twelfth to the twentieth century one sees the reason for this contrast. The initiative in producing this wonderful culture was not taken by the Church nor by religious enthusiasm as in the case of the first and real Christian civilization in the time of Constantine. It was a secular movement springing from the sudden and thorough emancipation of the human spirit, and originated with the laity. The Church at the beginning of this period was still the Church of the Dark Ages. Worldly-minded men had got control of it and were determined to hold that control. Uninfluenced by the changing spirit of the age they found themselves in opposition to the whole progressive movement that was forging a new, eager, active Europe. They would not tolerate the spirit of enquiry or the free use of reason. These they represented as being definitely heretical. Though Peter wrote (1 *Peter* iii 15) . . . "be ready always to give an answer to every man that asketh you a reason of the hope that is in you . . . ;" though Paul likewise wrote "Prove all things: hold fast that which is good" (1 *Thessalonians* v 21) and acted accordingly himself when "he reasoned in the synagogue every sabbath, and persuaded the Jews and the Greeks" (*Acts* xviii 4) and again when he "three sabbath days reasoned with them out of the scriptures" (*Acts* xvii 2); and though Jesus Christ Himself definitely taught men to use their reason to support their faith saying "*Wherefore, if God so clothe the grass of the field, which to-day is, and to-morrow is cast into the oven, shall he not much more clothe you, O ye of little faith?*" (*Matt.* vi 30), yet the religious authorities of those days (and many too of these days) regarded logic and investigation as wrong. They laid it down that the deposit of faith was static. It was once and for all delivered to the saints, and was not to be changed or challenged.

Under the reign of such views no Divine science, which might have balanced physical science and been to it a counterpart and equipoise, was ever able to arise. Verbalisms, sterile dogmas, riddles that might evoke controversy but could not illuminate the mind, took the place of a real search for spiritual truth, a real scrutiny of the deep mysteries of human and Divine nature. So inveterate was the hostility of the religious authorities of Christendom to the spirit of Truth and to the pursuit of knowledge that a careful historian wrote of it:

> "Until the seventeenth century, every mental disposition which philosophy pronounces to be essential to a legitimate research was almost uniformly branded as a sin, and a large proportion of the most deadly intellectual vices were deliberately inculcated as virtues. . . . In a word, there is . . . scarcely a rule which reason teaches as essential for its attainment, that theologians did not for centuries stigmatise as offensive to the Almighty."[1]

[1] Lecky, *History of the Rise and Influence of Rationalism in Europe*; chap. 4, part ii, pp. 87, 88. Longmans, London 1872.

The authorities supported their views by the use of persecution, the justification for which was based on the theory of the moral guilt of error.

'Abdu'l-Bahá once said that Reason was the throne of faith; in another place he likened Reason to a great mirror looking into the heavens but reflecting no image because it was in darkness. Faith, he said, was like sunlight which enabled the mirror to see and to reflect all the heavenly truths that lie before it. These symbols express exactly the Christian and the Bahá'í view of Reason and Faith, but not the view of traditional orthodoxy which is a purely human concept.

The whole position as regards heresy, dogma, enquiry, reason and the like was supported by the authority of a great institution, but Jesus had revealed no specific institution and all institutions, great and small, old or new, have been deduced by men's reason from this or that phrase or text of Gospel. No church to-day, or in any other day, can point to any statement in the Gospel which indicates its pattern, its rule of succession by which it can silence its critics. The whole system rests on sheer speculation. Not one of the institutions of Christendom can say it is designed and built in direct conformity with an express command of Christ in the Gospel. All are man-made.

Orthodoxy rather than detachment or moral righteousness has been the shibboleth of religious authorities. Their enthusiasm has been confined largely to insistence on teachings, doctrines, speculations which, like their own structure were devised by themselves, and around which controversies were raised which none could finally settle. About the main ethical injunctions of Christ and actual obedience to them there was no such insistence.

No church, for example, has ever adopted the challenging test for membership used by Jesus Himself for His disciples: "*By this shall all men know that ye are my disciples, if ye have love one to another.*" (*John* xiii 35).

Europe in consequence has never been tranquil, full of good will, united, but rather full of oppression, misery, strife and turbulence. The cause of Religion has been supported by the most flagrant breaches of Gospel ethics.

So far did the traditional religion of Europe, in its character and effects, differ from that of the Gospel, that it became the chief cause of unchristian feeling and behaviour. It promoted hatred and schism, discontent, strife, cruelty and injustice, suppression of truth and reason. It has conducted persecutions, burnings at the stake, extermination of heretics, suppression of truth by force. 'Abdu'l-Bahá comments on this subject in a talk given at Green Acre, Maine on August 17th, 1912: "*Nine hundred thousand martyrs to the protestant cause was the record of conflict and difference between that sect of Christians and the catholics. Consult history and confirm this.*"[1]

But now another divergence between the attitude of the Church and that of all progressives took shape and grew steadily more wide. The Church objected to that nation-building which had been the main contribution of Muḥammad to human history and which was to be as important to the building of Western civilization as it had been to Islám.

The interests of Church and State never were harmoniously combined in Christian history as they had been by Muḥammad. Four types of relationship have been essayed. First, that of Rome in which the Church

Promulgation of Universal Peace, Bahá'í Temple Unity, Chicago, 1922 (p. 259).

is above the State; second, that of Prussia in which the State is above the Church; third, that of England in which Church and State exist side by side as different aspects of one community; and lastly, that adopted in the United States of America where Church is regarded simply as a voluntary association of individuals and has no official relation to the nation at all.

Not one of these has been satisfactory. It has remained for the Bahá'í Faith alone to develop a structure of national life in which the two can be perfectly united and harmonized.

The development of the nation state has been in Europe a great modern feat, and its achievement has brought immense advantages to the advancement of science, the promotion of industry, the outlook of the ordinary man, and has given to the national life a freedom and a power not equalled by any earlier form of social structure. But these advantages have been won in spite of the Church and in our time the final result of the struggle is the humiliation of the Church and very often the secularization of the national life.

Not only has the prestige and influence of the Church been thus abased but the prestige and influence of religion with it; and at the same time materialism has been strengthened and exalted. The whole progress of our Western civilization has been, therefore, not the intensifying of Christianity but the opposite.

CHAPTER TEN

THE DAWN-SONG OF THE KINGDOM

ABOUT the beginning of the eighteenth century a new influence swept across Europe affecting the minds of all men. It showed itself in a spirit of confidence and enterprise, the sense of a new power. Hitherto men had tended to look back to the past and to old civilizations for the Golden Age, for their ideals and their models. Scholars, historians, religionists had looked back at Greece and Rome and Palestine, but now they looked rather at the present and at the future, seeking to make the world better, richer, fuller and to do this on their own initiative.

This was the age when the Industrial Revolution arose, changing the face of the world and the lives of men. Idealists dreamed of reform, seeking it not only in national terms but in universal. In all phases of life new hopes were born and sought fulfilment. As the century wore on indications of the origin and the meaning of this general impulse began to appear.

The Jews had, since the first and second centuries, territorially and politically ceased to be a nation, yet no people held more grimly to the sense of nationhood than they. Expelled from the Holy Land after the capture of Jerusalem in A.D. 70, under Titus, and again with more rigour about sixty years later under Hadrian, they were dispersed among nearly all the nations of the earth and they suffered every form of humiliation and misery for well-nigh sixteen centuries. But now in the eighteenth century for the first time a national life began to assert itself among them. It was the time for the Jewish Renaissance. In Europe and America nation after nation began to restore to them by slow degrees rights which for long centuries had been denied them. In 1723 Louis XV gave the Jews permission to hold real estate in France. In the same year England acknowledged them as English subjects. In 1738 Charles VI of Denmark opened all trades to the Jews. In 1750 Frederick II granted toleration to the Jews in his dominion. Joseph II of Austria in 1780 opened the schools and Universities of the Empire to the Jews, allowing them to follow any trade or establish manufacturing. In the year 1788 Louis XVI of France appointed a royal commission "to remodel on principles of justice all laws concerning the Jews." And so the tale goes on.

The United States of America was the first nation to embody in its laws the principle that Gentiles and Jews were equal in rights and privileges before the law (A.D. 1776).

The same process of gradual concession was continued through the nineteenth century, the year 1844 being a time of special importance, since in it the Turkish Government pledged to the Jews protection from persecution throughout the Ottoman Dominion, including of course the Holy Land, though it was not until 1867 that the Sublime Porte gave them the right to own real estate in the land of their fathers.

What could all this mean but the approach of the second coming of Christ?

Contemporary with this eighteenth century emancipation of the Jews there swept quietly into the minds of European men the impulsion of a new spiritual force, an impulsion the beginnings of which can hardly be traced but which gradually brought into men's minds a new spirit of hope and enterprise and happiness and creative vigour and which by steady gradations at the turn of the century and during the early years of the nineteenth century took the definite shape of the dawning on earth of a New Age, of the divinely-aided appearance of a new and better world, and in Christian circles of the return of Christ and the descent of the Kingdom of God from heaven.

The poet Wordsworth gives an excellent contemporary account of the new creative joy that mysteriously was wafted upon the world at that time, and of the confidence that possessed the hearts of men.

"Bliss was it in that dawn to be alive,
   But to be young was very Heaven ! O times, . . .
   When Reason seemed the most to assert her rights
   When most intent on making of herself
   A prime enchantress—to assist the work,
   Which then was going forward in her name !
   Not favoured spots alone, but the whole Earth,
   The beauty wore of promise—that which sets
   (As at some moments might not be unfelt
   Among the bowers of Paradise itself)
   The budding rose above the rose full blown.
   What temper at the prospect did not wake
   To happiness unthought of ? The inert
   Were roused, and lively natures rapt away ! . . .

Did now find helpers to their hearts' desire,
And stuff at hand, plastic as they could wish,—
Were called upon to exercise their skill,
Not in Utopia,—subterranean fields,—
Or some secreted island, Heaven knows where!
But in the very world, which is the world
Of all of us,—the place where, in the end,
We find our happiness, or not at all."

Prelude, Book XI and X[2]

But at the end of the eighteenth century and during the first decades of the nineteenth the intuitions of spiritual men spoke in clearer language. A burst of lyrical greetings welcomed the approaching coming of the Kingdom.

"The Night is ended and the Morning nears:
Awake, look up! I hear the gathering sound
Of coming cycles, like an ocean round;
I see the glory of a thousand years
Lightening from bound to bound."

Frederick Tennyson (1807–98)

"These things shall be: a loftier race
Than e'er the world hath known, shall rise,
With flame of freedom in their souls
And light of knowledge in their eyes . . .

"New arts shall bloom of loftier mould,
And mightier music thrill the skies,
And every life shall be a song
When all the earth is paradise."

J. A. Symonds (1840–93)

[1] See also Wordsworth's *Excursion*.

"The Day of the Lord is at hand, at hand:
  Its storms roll up the sky:
The nations sleep starving on heaps of gold;
  All dreamers toss and sigh;
The night is darkest before the morn;
When the pain is sorest the child is born,
    And the Day of the Lord is at hand. . . .

"Who would sit down and sigh for a lost age of gold,
  While the Lord of all ages is here?
True hearts will leap up at the trumpet of God,
  And those who can suffer, can dare.
Each old age of gold was an iron age too,
And the meekest of saints may find stern work to do,
    In the Day of the Lord at hand."

From Charles Kingsley's
The Day of the Lord, (written 1849).

The poets' enthusiasm crossed the Atlantic. It touched Whittier. It moved Julia Ward Howe to write, in 1861, the *Battle Hymn of the Republic*:

"Mine eyes have seen the glory of the coming of the
  Lord;
He is trampling out the vintage where the grapes of
  wrath are stored;
He hath loos'd the fateful lightning of His terrible
  swift sword,
His truth is marching on."

Apart from such verses stand apocalyptic works of Shelley; lyrics like the *Ode to the West Wind*, narratives such as *The Revolt of Islam* and especially his great poetical drama *Prometheus Unbound*, which many critics regard as the sublimest poem in the English language. Here in the poem the form of apocalypse does not appear, nor is any Christian imagery employed. The theme of the drama is verily and indeed that of the actual coming of the Kingdom. The hero is a godman who, moved by love and pity for mankind, in their ignorance and error and misery, through deliberate self-sacrifice and acute suffering for their sake, challenges and finally destroys the principle of evil, hurling into the abyss the Tyrant from his throne, thus redeeming permanently the human race. The very universe itself rejoices to share the universal regeneration of all living things.

Not poets alone but the generality of the people in town and in country, high and low, learned and un-learned, felt this new transcendent power stirring creation. The time was one of religious revival, of church building, of missionary expansion, the central motive being always the belief in the imminent coming of Christ.[1] For a full generation and more men and women everywhere dreamed, thought, talked and discussed this Advent. They met in church and chapel, in street and roadside, held assemblies and camp meetings that lasted far into the night. In many parts of England, in Southern Wales, in many parts of the United States from the East to the Middle West the fervour of the expectation spread. Adventist sects were started, a few of which remain to the present day, such as the Latter Day Saints and the Seventh Day Adventists. So strong was the feeling in one shape or another that the Messianic expectation lasted through the

[1] See the author's *The Promise of All Ages*, chap v.

whole of the nineteenth century and, reappearing in the apocalyptic sense of mission which has characterized communism and fascism, has tempted more dictators than one to regard themselves as Messianic beings.

For two centuries, it may perhaps be said, this new wave of power affected all the Western world except one section only, the institutions which claimed to be custodians of religious truth, which claimed to have a monopoly of keeping watch for Christ according to His command. The old established, historic churches of Christendom showed themselves irresponsive and uninterested. The false prophets had done their deadly work with full success. So misleading had been their interpretations of religious history that Christ had indeed come and no men had been so utterly ignorant of His presence as those who had appointed themselves to be His special guardians.

CHAPTER ELEVEN

THE BÁB[1]

THE Bible throughout has for its constant theme mankind's toilsome journey towards the Kingdom of God and paints its promised attainment with fervour and vividness and illimitable joy. These exquisite pictures have been for a hundred generations and more a source of undying comfort and happiness to a struggling race. But the Bible nowhere describes the inwardness of that Kingdom nor develops the psychology of it, nor explains why the Kingdom should come at that particular stage of man's journey. Jesus admits expressly that He had other things to say and gives as His reason for withholding the knowledge that mankind in His day was not advanced and mature enough to understand its future experiences.

But now the Herald of the Kingdom had come and gone. The Seal of the Prophets had likewise come and gone. The next great spiritual event was the actual coming of the Kingdom which both these Revelators had announced.

With the Báb the Kingdom actually begins. He stands both as a Revealer Prophet bringing His own Dispensation and Laws and also as a Forerunner of One, Bahá'u'lláh, bearing a Revelation immeasurably greater than His own.

[1] Siyyid 'Alí-Muḥammad of Shíráz, a descendant of Muḥammad, known to history as the Báb. 1819-50. He was the Qá'im of Islám and Fore-runner of Bahá'u'lláh, "*He Whom God should manifest.*"

Standing at the close of the whole Prophetic Cycle[1] His Revelation is described as including twenty-five out of the twenty-seven letters of all knowledge; and with Him each and every past Prophet has a separate Covenant, concerning the One whom He heralded, the Supreme World Redeemer. Thus He stands at the confluence of the Prophetic Cycle which is closed and of the Age of Fulfilment which now opens. The Bahá'í Era begins with His Declaration on the evening of May 22nd, 1844, and ushers in the universal Age of Truth. The creative energies which He imparts endow mankind with the capacity to attain its maturity which will enable it in course of time and in conjunction with the still greater power generated by Bahá'u'lláh to achieve the organic unification of the human race.

To any spiritually expectant soul, the Báb's declaration would have indicated that the Kingdom of God had indeed come. No earlier Manifestation, not even Jesus Christ Himself had issued a challenge to the rulers of the world proclaiming the Self-Sufficiency of His Cause, denouncing the vanity of their ephemeral power and calling upon them to lay aside, one and all, their dominion, and deliver His Message to lands in both the East and the West. But to such men as the Persian authorities, such claims merely proved the Author was an undoubted mountebank and probably not in his right mind and that His Cause would quickly collapse of its own weight.

The progress of the Báb's teaching never kept pace with the ardour of His own desire. His pilgrimage to Mecca bore no visible fruit, and upon His return He, Himself,

---

[1] Muḥammad, the "Seal of the Prophets" was the last Prophet in the Age of Promise; the Báb closed that Age and opened the Age of Fulfilment.

was arrested and brought under escort to Shíráz where He was violently buffeted in open court and released only on parole. His disciples carrying His Message through the country were everywhere opposed and often manhandled and persecuted. Some were tortured and some killed.

But at the same time the fire of the Bábís kindled interest and enthusiasm through the countryside and the bazaars. The Báb's own eloquence and radiant charm warmed the hearts of many. And when the upper officials of Church and State, at the end of two years and more, took stock of the situation they found that the Báb had captivated the hearts of high and low in the important Shí'ih city of Iṣfáhán and that His Cause was now spreading among the merchant class, through the Army and the landed gentry. Thoroughly alarmed at the result of their slackness, they formed a carefully designed plan which they would pursue remorselessly till this monstrous heresy (as they thought it) had been stamped out.

In 1847 the Báb was carried to the lonely mountain fastness of Ádhírbáyján and there imprisoned first in the castle of Máh-Kú and then in that of Chihríq, where He spent the short remainder of His life. Shí'ih Mullás denounced His teachings and from their pulpits incited their congregations against all Bábís, appealing to their fanaticism. Bábís were assaulted, their houses entered and spoiled, their women maltreated. The courts gave no protection, no redress. The Bábís were practically outlawed.

In three neighbourhoods, those of Ṭabarsí, of Nayríz and of Zanján, the Bábís stood at bay and were only overcome by the King's troops using perjury and treachery as well as overwhelming numbers.

Deeply angered by the cruel imprisonment of their

beloved Lord, the Bábís fought back in His name with such success that the new Prime Minister resolved to end this conflict at once by putting the Báb to death, with or without legal warrant. The Báb was brought from Chihríq to Tabríz where He was shot to death.

The occasion of His martyrdom provides the spiritual history of martyrdom with an undoubted miracle, attested by witnesses on both sides.[1] The Báb was suspended by a rope to a beam let into the prison wall, a favoured disciple being suspended across His breast. A Christian regiment was chosen to be the firing force and its colonel, horrified at the thought of raising his hand against so holy a Man, implored Him to excuse him from committing so great a sacrilege. *"Follow your instructions,"* said the Báb, *"and if your intention be sincere, the Almighty is surely able to relieve you from your perplexity."*

Just before the execution the Báb drew aside His amanuensis, Siyyid Husayn, for a confidential conversation in one of the rooms of the prison. The gaoler interrupted and ordered the Báb to go at once. *"Not until I have said to him all those things that I wish to say,"* the Báb warned the gaoler, *"can any earthly power silence Me. Though all the world be armed against Me, yet shall they be powerless to deter Me from fulfilling, to the last word, My intention."* He then went with the gaoler.

The Christian regiment opened fire at the Báb and His disciple, tied to the beam of wood, and when the smoke from seven hundred and fifty rifles had cleared away, it was seen by ten thousand onlookers that the Báb had disappeared and the disciple was standing unharmed, on

---

[1] A. L. M. Nicolas *Siyyid 'Alí-Muhammad dit le Báb*, p. 375-9
The Dawnbreakers, Nabíl's Narrative, ch xxiii.

the ground. A frantic search ensued and the Báb was discovered completing His talk with His amanuensis. *"I have finished my conversation with Siyyid Ḥusayn,"* He said, *"Now you may proceed to fulfil your intention."*

The Christian regiment refused to continue the execution. Their place was taken by Muslims and the Báb and His disciple were instantly killed.

Their bodies were thrown out in a moat but rescued by the disciples and now they rest in the Holy Land in a beautiful mausoleum built by thousands of believers from all parts of the world.

The Bábís refused to be discouraged, even by the execution of their Lord, and continued to make converts to His Cause.

Two years later an effort to assassinate the Sháh was made by two obscure and irresponsible youths and this gave the priests the excuse they were looking for. Throughout the whole of Persia the Bábís were hunted out and hounded down, and the ordeal of torture and massacre did not cease till the soil of Persia was incarnadined with the blood of martyrs and the authorities felt absolutely assured that the Faith of the Báb was dead and could never rise again.

CHAPTER TWELVE

BAHÁ'U'LLÁH

BAHÁ'U'LLÁH was descended from Abraham by His wife Katurah, thus fulfilling the prophecy to Abraham that in Him would all the families of the earth be blessed.

It is difficult for an English reader to learn much about Bahá'u'lláh's early days. We know, however, that He was born on 12th November, 1817, two years before the Báb. From His early days He showed signs of wonder and power. His father dreamed a dream of Him while He was yet a child, which is recounted by Nabíl.

"Bahá'u'lláh appeared to him swimming in a vast, limitless ocean. His body shone upon the waters with a radiance that illumined the sea. Around His head, which could distinctly be seen above the waters, there radiated, in all directions, His long, jet-black locks, floating in great profusion above the waves. As he dreamed, a multitude of fishes gathered round Him, each holding fast to the extremity of one hair. Fascinated by the effulgence of His face, they followed Him in whatever direction He swam. Great as was their number, and however firmly they clung to His locks, not one single hair seemed to have been detached from His head, nor did the least injury affect His person. Free and unrestrained, He moved above the waters and they all followed Him.

"The Vazír,[1] greatly impressed by this dream, summoned a soothsayer, who had achieved fame in that region, and asked him to interpret it for him. This man, as if inspired by a premonition of the future glory of Bahá'u'lláh, declared: 'The limitless ocean that you have seen in your dream, O Vazír, is none other than the world of being. Singlehanded and alone, your son will achieve supreme ascendancy over it. Wherever He may please, He will proceed unhindered. No one will resist His march, no one will hinder His progress. The multitude of fishes signifies the turmoil which He will arouse amidst the peoples and kindreds of the earth. Around Him will they gather, and to Him will they cling. Assured of the unfailing protection of the Almighty, this tumult will never harm His person, nor will His loneliness upon the sea of life endanger His safety.' "[2]

Bahá'u'lláh loved people, especially children. He loved to be surrounded by them and they loved Him. From childhood He delighted in country life, in trees, in flowers and horseback riding.

He came of a noble and wealthy family which had long been prominent in the political sphere and He Himself was endowed with a gift of eloquence like a rushing torrent. As the years passed on He showed no inclination for political affairs but spent His time in looking after the needy, the poor and the sick. When His father died He succeeded to the management of a large estate and married the daughter of a well-known vazír. Her tastes resembled His and they became known as the Father of the Poor and the Mother of Consolation.

---

[1] Bahá'u'lláh's father.

[2] *The Dawnbreakers*, Nabíl's Narrative, chap v.

One day, when He was twenty-seven years old, a
messenger brought Him a package containing a manuscript which had been written by the Báb and sent by the
hand of His first disciple, Mullá Ḥusayn. From this
document He learned that the Kingdom of God, so long
expected by the devout, had indeed at last come, that the
Báb had declared Himself its Prophet and was sending out
through Persia His messengers to announce the breaking
of the new Day. The document was none other than some
pages of the Qayyúmu'l-Asmá, the "*first, greatest and
mightiest*" of the Báb's works, the first chapter of which
He had revealed on the night of His declaration. In it He
called on the Sháh and the kings and princes of the earth
to acknowledge His station and He called even the people
of the West to come forth and welcome Him.

On reading a portion of this manuscript Bahá'u'lláh
at once discerned that the spiritual note of the writing was
the same as that of the Qur'án and He accepted its
message. Casting aside at once all thought of His personal
interest, regardless of His wealth, of His social eminence,
of His youth, of His talents and of the brilliant future
open before Him, He espoused the Cause of an obscure
merchant[1] and began to serve it with the utmost ardour.
Though He must long before have realized the divinity of
the station which really belonged to Himself, Bahá'u'lláh
promptly joined the Báb's followers and never disclosed
His own true rank to anyone.

During the years of the Báb's Ministry He showed Himself a loyal and devoted coadjutor, not only by His outstanding character and His extraordinary ability but also by His
heart-whole enthusiasm and personal devotion to the Báb.

[1] The Báb was a wool-merchant, with His uncle in Shíráz.

The two Prophets never met on this earth but kept in the closest touch by letter and otherwise. Both were to suffer for the Cause and vied with one another in doing so. Three times Bahá'u'lláh was scourged as a Bábí, three times imprisoned, and the Báb in His turn three times suffered the same punishments. After the Conference at Badasht Muḥammad Sháh determined to put Bahá'u'lláh to death, but died too soon to carry out his threat. It was to Bahá'u'lláh that the Báb sent His most precious personal possessions (His pen and His ring) when He felt His martyrdom was drawing near, and it was Bahá'u'lláh Who, on the night of the Báb's execution, arranged for some of the disciples to carry away the body from the moat into which it had been thrown and to conceal it in a safe place of hiding.

At the time of the attempt on the Sháh's life Bahá'u'lláh was staying at Lavásán as the guest of the Grand Vizír. Rejecting the protection and the good offices tendered Him, Bahá'u'lláh went to the headquarters of the Imperial Army at Níyávarán and was conducted thence under escort and in chains, bareheaded and with bare feet to Ṭihrán. There He was taken at once to the Síyáh-Chál, the most terrible of all the dungeons in the capital.

Bahá'u'lláh in His *Epistle to the Son of the Wolf* gives the following description of the place in which He found Himself: "*The dungeon was wrapt in thick darkness, and Our fellow-prisoners numbered nearly a hundred and fifty souls: thieves, assassins and highwaymen. Though crowded, it had no other outlet than the passage by which We entered. No pen can depict that place, nor any tongue describe its loathsome smell. Most of these men had neither clothes nor bedding to lie on. God alone knoweth what befell Us in that most foul-smelling and gloomy place!"* (pp. 20-21).

Such was the place and such the occasion which God chose for the Call of Bahá'u'lláh to the office of Prophethood, and to the assumption of His Ministry.

An independent Prophet has two stations: one a divine and the other a human station. His essential being is divine. As such He is the Word of God. The Kitáb-i-Íqán states of these Beings that: *"These sanctified Mirrors, these Day-springs of ancient glory are one and all the Exponents on earth of Him Who is the central Orb of the universe, its Essence and ultimate Purpose. From Him proceed their knowledge and power; from Him is derived their sovereignty. The beauty of their countenance is but a reflection of His image, and their revelation a sign of His deathless glory. They are the Treasuries of divine knowledge, and the Repositories of celestial wisdom. Through them is transmitted a grace that is infinite, and by them is revealed the light that can never fade."* (pp. 99-100)

And again in the same book it is written, *"These ancient Beings, though delivered from the womb of their mother, have in reality descended from the heaven of the will of God. Though they be dwelling on this earth, yet their true habitations are the retreats of glory in the realms above. Whilst walking amongst mortals, they soar in the heaven of the divine presence. Without feet they tread the path of the spirit, and without wings they rise unto the exalted heights of divine unity. With every fleeting breath they cover the immensity of space, and at every moment traverse the kingdoms of the visible and the invisible. . . . They are sent forth through the transcendent power of the Ancient of Days, and are raised up by the exalted will of God, the most mighty King. This is what is meant by the words: 'coming in the clouds of heaven' "* (p. 67, U.S. ed.).

But they undergo a very definite, moving and tremendous experience when God wills that their Mission should open and the full power of the sovereignty which belongs to them shall be disclosed. Every Prophet goes through this experience and often finds it altogether overwhelming. We read of Moses falling into a swoon, and of Muḥammad running to His home and imploring His wife, Khadíjih, to envelop Him in His mantle. The experience alters altogether the relation between Almighty God and the Prophet, but does not necessarily make any difference between the Prophet and the people until the Prophet Himself so elects. Jesus Himself, for instance, is thought to have been called to His Ministry at the time of His baptism by John in Jordan, but He did not openly declare Himself till His pronouncement to the Jewish Sanhedrin on the last night of His life.

Bahá'u'lláh describes this Call in the following words in His letter to the Sháh: "*O King! I was but a man like others, asleep upon My couch, when lo, the breezes of the All-Glorious were wafted over Me, and taught Me the knowledge of all that hath been. This thing is not from Me, but from One Who is Almighty and All-Knowing. And He bade Me lift up My voice between earth and heaven, and for this there befell Me what hath caused the tears of every man of understanding to flow. . . . This is but a leaf which the winds of the will of Thy Lord, the Almighty, the All-Praised, have stirred.*"

Many years later, in His *Epistle to the Son of the Wolf* He tells how, "*One night, in a dream, these exalted words were heard on every side: 'Verily, We shall render Thee victorious by Thyself and by Thy pen. Grieve Thou not for that which hath befallen Thee, neither be Thou afraid, for Thou art in*

*safety. Ere long will God raise up the treasures of the earth—
men who will aid Thee through Thyself and through Thy
Name, wherewith God hath revived the hearts of such as have
recognized Him'* " (p. 21).

'Abdu'l-Bahá pointed out that the Prophet's experience
when this call comes to Him is purely physical. There is
no change of the Prophet's individuality. He remains
precisely the same.[1]

Thus it was that Bahá'u'lláh's Ministry began in the
year 9 (1853 A.D., 1269 A.H.) as the Báb had already
indicated, a time which imbued the whole world with
unimaginable potentialities. The attempt on the life of the
Sháh had taken place on 15th August, 1852; Bahá'u'lláh
had been thrown into the Síyáh-Chál almost immediately
afterwards and about the middle of October this Divine
Call had come, endowing Him with the fullness of the
power of the sovereignty which went with His Divine
Mission. Two months later He was proved innocent of
any connection with the crime, having been strongly
defended by His friends and by the Russian Ambassador.

Delivered from the Síyáh-Chál Bahá'u'lláh found
Himself still the prisoner of the Sháh, reduced almost to
destitution by the confiscation of all His property and
under sentence of banishment from His native land to
Baghdád in 'Iráq whither He was to start within one
month.

During the ten years He spent in Baghdád His fame and
personal influence reached their highest point. So great
was His influence that by degrees He spread among the
Bábís cheer and hope and confidence in their Faith, not
only in His neighbourhood but even among the lonely

[1] *Some Answered Questions*, chap. xxxix.

hamlets of Persia. Still acting as a Bábí and without going beyond the Báb's teachings, He made the Faith more universal than it had been before, and bringing into prominence higher teachings of the Báb, long disused, lifted the religion to a higher level. His intuitive understanding of scripture astonished and attracted Bábí pilgrims from all directions and also drew eager Muslim students from Karbilá and Najaf. His modest home became the constant resort of enquirers on spiritual matters. That same unique Spirit of Divine Love which suffused so much of His writings was felt by His companions in its original intensity and won Him their love and devotion to a degree which chroniclers of the time record. Joyous feasts celebrating their love for Him were held, in spite of poverty, and many writings still testify to His little parlour being felt as an avenue to Paradise such as men's hearts had never known before. The ethical level of the Bábí community was exalted beyond recognition and the good name of the Faith began to extend itself in all directions. His great religious revelation, the *Book of Certitude*,[1] written in Baghdád, summarizes in two hundred pages the grand universal scheme of Redemption and explains not only the great central truths of God's revealing method but those difficulties of interpretation which have always caused discord among the great religious systems of the world.

So rapid was Bahá'u'lláh's ascent to heights of brilliance and spiritual power that the ecclesiastical authorities of such neighbouring cities as Karbilá were moved to bitter jealousy and took counsel together how to get rid of Him. They represented that He was still too near Persia to be a

[1] Persian *Kitáb-i-Íqán*.

harmless neighbour and persuaded the Sháh that He should be removed further away, and by degrees brought pressure on Turkish officials to keep Him under stricter surveillance. Bahá'u'lláh's undoubted influence among the people and many leaders of opinion in Baghdád made Him open to suspicion of personal designs. By 1863 His enemies had secured His sentence of exile to Constantinople.

Ten years had now elapsed since the time of His Call and the time was ripe for an open declaration of the power and sovereignty which for so long had been flooding His soul. On the 21st April, for a period of twelve days, Bahá'u'lláh, in the beautiful Najíbíyyih garden on the river banks outside Baghdád, instituted the great Feast of Riḍván which is held as the most joyous and triumphant of all Bahá'í Feasts. He assumed before His followers and the wide world the supreme authority which He had received from the Most High at the time of His Call. Now it was that Jesus Christ ascended His throne in the power of God the Father. Now it was that He took upon Himself the sceptre of the fullness of God's might and thus set Himself as Supreme Overlord of all that is in heaven and on earth.

The significance of that Feast for Himself and for the world is expressed by His calling it *"the King of Festivals,"* *"the Day of God."* In His own greatest work the *Aqdas*[1] He characterizes it as the Day whereon *"all created things were immersed in the sea of purification."* In another Tablet He refers to it as the day whereon *"the breezes of forgiveness were wafted over the entire creation."* And again He writes, *"Rejoice with exceeding gladness, O people of Bahá, as ye call*

[1] *Kitáb-i-Aqdas.*

to remembrance the Day of supreme felicity, the Day whereon the Tongue of the Ancient of Days hath spoken, as He departed from His House, proceeding to the Spot from which He shed upon the whole of creation the splendours of His Name, the All-Merciful."

Surely this Day must be the greatest day in the history of mankind.

CHAPTER THIRTEEN

THE PROCLAMATION TO THE KINGS

IMMEDIATELY after His Declaration at Riḍván, Bahá'-
u'lláh and His party set out on the long journey to
Constantinople. Here they remained only four months,
the Sulṭán sending them in mid-winter and in the most
severe conditions on a third journey into exile. In
Adrianople Bahá'u'lláh remained about four years and in
1868 was sent on His fourth and last exile, this time to
'Akká, the dungeon city of which it was said the very
birds fell dead as they passed over it.

It was during this period and chiefly during His
residence in Adrianople that Bahá'u'lláh proclaimed in
great Tablets His station and His mission to the rulers
of the world. Some of these are of especial moment to
Western and Christian readers; first His Tablet to the
Kings of the earth collectively, issued in 1864, and secondly
His individual Tablets to the four chief monarchs of
Europe. The first of these is described by the Guardian[1]
as the most momentous of all His Tablets,[2] and in it He
summons all the kings and the ecclesiastical rulers of the
world to turn to Him and follow his dictates. What
sublimer exordium could there be to such a document
than this:

[1] The Guardian of the Bahá'í Faith, Shoghi Effendi, Bahá'u'lláh's great-
grandson. See chap. 15.

[2] *Súriy-i-Mulúk.*

*"O Kings of the earth! Give ear unto the Voice of God . . .
intoning the words: 'There is none other God but He, the
Mighty, the All-Powerful, the All-Wise.' . . . Fear God, O
concourse of kings, and suffer not yourselves to be deprived of
this most sublime grace. Fling away, then, the things ye possess,
and take fast hold on the Handle of God, the Exalted, the Great.
Set your hearts towards the Face of God, and abandon that
which your desires have bidden you to follow, and be not of those
who perish."*

Bahá'u'lláh then tells them of the martyrdom of the
Báb by the unjust and cruel divines of Persia. He holds
them one and all responsible for this crime and requires
that they make amends for it. He demands that they follow
that which He speaks unto them, with their hearts, and
calls on them to arise and set themselves towards the Holy
Court of God.

Bahá'u'lláh made it clear He was going to establish the
Kingdom of God throughout the world; but He did not
ask the kings to give Him any aid whatsoever in the
task. What He did ask was that they should consider that
their glory consisted in obedience to God, not in the
width or wealth of their dominions; that they should rule
their subjects with the utmost nicety of justice, should
regard the poor among them as a particular trust from
God; that they should reduce taxation and heal their
dissensions till they were able to do without armies and
their expensive upkeep except for police purposes.

Unless they obeyed the directions of this kind which He
gave, He warned them that assuredly calamities, heavy
and many, would descend upon them from every direction; they would not be able to escape but would be
caught and overwhelmed.

For Himself, He demanded that the kings should scrutinize the wrongs which He and His had had to endure through twenty years and judge justly between Him and His enemies.

He assured the kings that God had promised to exalt His Cause even if no king on earth helped Him.

This call, however, (which as He expressly stated was that of the Most Great Peace) was immediately and with disdain rejected by the kings, one and all.

By an act of forgiveness Bahá'u'lláh made to the Christian kings of Europe a further offer. He addressed to the Emperor Napoleon III of France, to Pope Pius IX, to Queen Victoria and to Czar Alexander, individual letters in which He asked of them their aid in establishing God's Kingdom among the nations. Napoleon was at the moment the most powerful and brilliant of the European sovereigns and to him Bahá'u'lláh offered the leadership in this great undertaking. He called on Napoleon to introduce the new Revelation and told him that the clergy who held to the old worship and refused the new would be as fallen stars and lose their status and authority. He revealed to Napoleon several of the great new principles of the new Faith; explained the succession of religions, Islám succeeding Christianity, Christianity succeeding Mosaism, Moses succeeding Abraham. He stated that His own Mission was to regenerate and to unify the whole human race, which was to be regarded as one great family, in fact as one individual, as one soul in many bodies. He asserted that force, which had so long been used in teaching, must be abandoned, and methods of persuasion and wisdom only should be used; and that effective teaching would depend on the single-hearted sincerity of the teacher. He said that the monks were to leave their monasteries, to marry and mingle with the life of the people; and celibacy was not and never had been approved by the Almighty as a better way of life than marriage.

He called on Napoleon to give up his crown, or if he retained it, to use it only for the service of God, and promised to assure the success of Napoleon in carrying out His, Bahá'u'lláh's programme. He would be regarded as king of the world.

At the same time He told Napoleon that he had shown insincerity and insolence; retribution was pursuing him and if he delayed in obeying Bahá'u'lláh, he would be utterly humiliated and overthrown and would lose everything.

Napoleon's rejoinder was a contemptuous refusal. Within a year he was defeated at Sedan and lost his empire and his throne.

Bahá'u'lláh announced to Pope Pius IX "*He Who is the Lord of Lords is come,*" and he who is the Rock (meaning Peter), crieth out "*Lo, the Father is come, and that which ye were promised in the Kingdom is fulfilled.*" He bade him "*Arise in the name of thy Lord, the God of Mercy, amidst the peoples of the earth, and seize thou the Cup of Life with the hands of confidence, and first drink thou therefrom, and proffer it then to such as turn towards it amongst the peoples of all faiths. . . . sell all the embellished ornaments thou dost possess and expend them in the path of God. . . . Abandon thy kingdom unto the kings, and emerge from thy habitation . . . speak forth the praises of thy Lord betwixt earth and heaven.*"

Bahá'u'lláh added an appeal couched in language of the warmest love and longing to the followers of Christ, urging them to recognize and flock into the Kingdom of God which others were already entering though they had not the first right to it.

The Pope ignored the letter altogether, and the following year by a stroke less spectacular than that which befell Napoleon, but equally significant, was by force deprived of the temporal rule which he had refused to surrender voluntarily, and became the prisoner of the Vatican.

Thus the year 1870 may be regarded as marking the disruption and decline of Western civilization.

To Queen Victoria Bahá'u'lláh revealed that the Gospel prophecies were fulfilled in His advent and He offered her a prayer exquisitely tender in its feeling which she might use in turning to Him as He admonished her to do. He commended her for two measures which had been recently adopted in the spirit of the new age, one the stoppage of the slave-trade, the other the extension of the franchise. He wrote at some length to her on the divine art of government, tracing historically the causes of its failure and indicating that it was now in a dangerous condition.

Through her He sent a reprimand to the kings for refusing the Most Great Peace and urgently advised them to adopt the Lesser Peace which would in some degree better their condition.

His fourth letter, addressed to Czar Alexander II was couched in warm language and He advised the Czar to arise and make known this Cause to the nations of the world.

It is reported that Queen Victoria, on reading His letter, remarked, "If this is of God, it will stand. Otherwise it

can do no harm." But neither she nor any of the other
Christian rulers turned to Him, nor paid any heed whatever to His counsels.

He remarked of them that they were intoxicated
with pride, unable to see what was best for their own
material interest, much less to recognize so stupendous a
Revelation.

Bahá'u'lláh had now been rejected by all the rulers of
the world and His removal to 'Akká cut Him off completely from active touch with world affairs. It should be
noted, however, that in exiling Him to 'Akká, the Holy
Land, the Sulṭán had fulfilled the ancient prophecy to the
effect that the Lord of Hosts would give His Revelation
there and thus made it impossible for anyone to say that
Bahá'u'lláh had fulfilled the prophecy of His own free
will.

Bahá'u'lláh's trust in the Christians and in their support
of His teachings never weakened. Towards the end of His
life He wrote the Holy Tablet,[1] an important work
addressed to them in which He rebukes them for their
slowness in recognizing Him, promises He will be faithful
and pours forth a succession of enthusiastic beatitudes on
the Christians, who will turn to Him with loving hearts
and serve His Faith.

About the same time Professor Edward Granville
Browne, of Cambridge University, came in touch with
the light of the Báb, became His life-long admirer and
pursued a vigorous research of the Báb's history which
led him in the end to 'Akká where he was received by
Bahá'u'lláh and was thus enabled to write, in that famous
introduction to *A Traveller's Narrative*:

[1] *Lawḥ-i-Aqdas.*

"The face of him on whom I gazed I can never forget, though I cannot describe it. Those piercing eyes seemed to read one's very soul; power and authority sat on that ample brow; while the deep lines on the forehead and face implied an age which the jet-black hair and beard flowing down in indistinguishable luxuriance almost to the waist seemed to belie. No need to ask in whose presence I stood, as I bowed myself before one who is the object of a devotion and love which kings might envy and emperors sigh for in vain!"[1]

And that other quotation from the lips of Bahá'u'lláh Himself which, when quoted at the world parliament of religions in Chicago in 1893, proved to be the instrument of bringing Bahá'u'lláh's Revelation to the knowledge of the Western world. The words were spoken to Browne during the interview with Bahá'u'lláh in 'Akká.

"*Thou hast come to see a prisoner and an exile. . . . We desire but the good of the world and the happiness of the nations; yet they deem us a stirrer up of strife and sedition worthy of bondage and banishment. . . . That all nations should become one in faith and all men as brothers; that the bonds of affection and unity between the sons of men should be strengthened; that diversity of religion should cease, and difference of race be annulled—what harm is there in this? . . . Yet so it shall be; these fruitless strifes, these ruinous wars shall pass away, and the 'Most Great Peace' shall come. . . . Do not you in Europe need this also? Is not this that which Christ foretold? . . . Yet do we see your kings and rulers lavishing their treasures more freely on means for the destruction of the human race*

[1] E. G. Browne, *A Traveller's Narrative*, Introduction. Cambridge.

than on that which would conduce to the happiness of mankind . . . These strifes and this bloodshed and discord must cease, and all men be as one kindred and one family... Let not a man glory in this, that he loves his country; let him rather glory in this, that he loves his kind. . . ."[1]

Bahá'u'lláh passed away in 1892. Communication between America and 'Akká began soon after 1893 and before the end of the century American pilgrims began to arrive after a difficult and uncertain journey, by way of the sea, at the prison city where 'Abdu'l-Bahá, Son of Bahá'u'lláh, was still immured.

[1] ibid.

CHAPTER FOURTEEN

'ABDU'L-BAHÁ

B AHÁ'U'LLÁH appointed in His written Will His son 'Abdu'l-Bahá as His successor and with this successorship joined powers to which no successor of any earlier Prophet had attained and which give 'Abdu'l-Bahá a position altogether unique in religious history. Bahá'u'lláh designated Him as the Centre and pivot of His peerless Covenant; as the perfect mirror of His life, to exemplify His teachings; as the unerring interpreter of His Word; as the embodiment of every Bahá'í ideal and virtue.

Bahá'u'lláh called Him the Mystery of God and wrote further of Him, "*a Word hath, as a token of Our grace, gone forth from the Most Great Tablet—a Word which God hath adorned with the ornament of His own Self, and made it sovereign over the earth and all that is therein, and a sign of His greatness and power among its people. . . . Render thanks unto God, O people, for His appearance; for verily He is the most great Favour unto you, the most perfect bounty upon you; and through Him every mouldering bone is quickened.*"

Such was He who was now to give a large part of His time and effort to the service of the Christian West.

'Abdu'l-Bahá was the age-fellow of the Bahá'í Faith; He had been born on the same evening as the Declaration of the Báb; had been the first to recognize, at the age of nine, the exalted transformation of Bahá'u'lláh after His

Call, and had gone at the same time into exile with His Father. In 1868 He entered with His Father the Most Great Prison of 'Akká, remaining in captivity for forty years till the Young Turk Revolution in the year 1908 gave Him His liberty. In 1910, although in poor health owing to His prison suffering, He set out to visit the West, and made two tours occupying three years. His chief addresses given at this time are recorded in *The Promulgation of Universal Peace* (Talks in America), *Paris Talks* and *'Abdu'l-Bahá in London*.

As He knew well, the position of the West at this time was already one of great danger, although the Christians of the West had no idea whatever of the retribution that was confronting them. 'Abdu'l-Bahá has briefly explained what had happened in one of His Tablets which begins with the following lines:

"O Army of Life! East and West have joined to worship stars of faded splendour, and have turned in prayer unto darkened horizons. Both have utterly neglected the broad foundation of God's sacred laws, and have grown unmindful of the merits and virtues of His religion. They have regarded certain customs and conventions as the basis of the Divine faith, and have firmly established themselves therein. They have imagined themselves as having attained a glorious pinnacle of achievement and prosperity, when in reality they have touched the innermost depths of heedlessness and deprived themselves wholly of God's bounteous gifts."

The people of Europe and America whom He addressed were not only completely oblivious of their real condition as seen by Him, but held the very opposite opinion. They were assured that the great and mighty civilization of the Christian West was due to their own effort, and that it was the final product of all civilizations of the past, of the Greek and Roman and that of Persia and India and China and Egypt, which had been preparatory only. They had no doubt that they at this time were the most enlightened generation of the most enlightened age the world had ever known. Physical science had, they thought, reached the limit of reality and probed all the problems and in fact knew all that was to be known. White man in the plenitude of his power was now established in material control of the weaker nations of the world and would hold the economic, military and political domination of the world indefinitely.

Some such views as these were probably held by every educated person in audiences to whom 'Abdu'l-Bahá spoke in the West; more particularly by those in England; and that such views of the achievements of the Western mind prevailed twenty years or more after 'Abdu'l-Bahá's visit will be suggested by the following quotation from a famous historical work by a brilliant and illustrious Oxford scholar:

"Our civilization, then, is distinct: it is also all-pervading and preponderant. In superficial area Europe is surpassed by Asia, Africa, and America, in population by the vast stable peasantry of Asia, which outnumbers not Europe only, but the rest of the world put together. Yet if a comprehensive survey of the globe were to be made, it would be found that in almost every quarter of it there were settlements of European men, or traces of the operation of the European mind. The surviving aboriginal peoples in the western hemisphere are a small, unimportant, and dwindling element in the

population. The African negroes have been introduced by white men as an economic convenience.
Northern and southern America are largely popu-
lated by colonists from Europe. Australasia is British.
The political direction of Africa has fallen, with the
ambiguous exception of the lower reaches of the Nile,
into European hands. In Asia the case is not dissimilar.
The political influences of Europe are apparent, even
where they are not, as in India or Palestine, em-
bodied in direct European control. The ideas of
nationality and responsible government, of freedom
and progress, of democracy and democratic education, have passed from the west to the east with
revolutionary and far-reaching consequences.

"It is, moreover, to European man that the world
owes the incomparable gifts of modern science. To
the conquest of nature through knowledge the
contributions made by Asiatics have been negligible
and by Africans (Egyptians excluded) non-existent.
The printing press and the telescope, the steam-
engine, the internal combustion engine and the
aeroplane, the telegraph and telephone, wireless
broadcasting and the cinematograph, the gramophone
and television, together with all the leading dis-
coveries in physiology, the circulation of the blood,
the laws of respiration and the like, are the result
of researches carried out by white men of European
stock. It is hardly excessive to say that the material fab-
ric of modern civilized life is the result of the intellectual daring and tenacity of the European peoples."[1]

[1] H. A. L. Fisher, *A History of Europe*, Introduction pp. 1, 2. Edward Arnold
& Co., London, 1936.

'Abdu'l-Bahá, of course, knew that such opinions of the importance of Western civilization were utterly and cruelly illusive. He knew that the Báb had called on the peoples of the West to come forth from their cities and aid the Cause of God, warning all humanity of the *"most terrible, the most grievous vengeance of God"*; that Bahá'u'lláh had said that the time for the destruction of the world and its people had arrived. *"The days are approaching their end, and yet the peoples of the earth are seen sunk in grievous heedlessness, and lost in manifest error." "Great, great is the Cause! The hour is approaching when the most great convulsion will have appeared. I swear by Him Who is the Truth! It shall cause separation to afflict every one, even those who circle around Me." "Say, O concourse of the heedless! I swear by God! The promised day is come, the day when tormenting trials will have surged above your heads, and beneath your feet, saying: 'Taste ye what your hands have wrought!'" "The day is approaching when its* (civilization's) *flame will devour the cities, when the Tongue of Grandeur will proclaim: 'The Kingdom is God's, the Almighty, the All-Praised!'"*

He knew that Bahá'u'lláh had declared that divine chastisement would assail the kings of the earth. He knew from the sudden doom of the Emperor Napoleon III and of the Pope, a year after the warnings given them, how sudden and terrible this retribution might be. And the Christian Bible was the accepted authority as to the coming of the Kingdom of God and of the great events that should be associated with it, and He was not likely to forget the pronouncements of horror and doom and the abasement of man's pride that according to prophets like Isaiah, Joel, Zechariah and many another were to be among the signs of the Day of the Lord. Nor would He forget how, by prophets like Ezekiel, terrible warfare and vast carnage were foretold as preceding the final victory of God on earth. He would not forget the prediction of Jesus that affliction such as the world had never known would precede that victory and that no flesh would be saved unless the time were shortened. In the book of *Revelation* the hosts of righteousness are shown as being led by Christ against the hosts of evil and the awfulness of the bloodshed that would ensue is dramatically portrayed by pictures of the wine vats flowing blood-red with the blood of the grapes.

All these Bible prophecies agreed in large and in little with the events that were now taking shape through the Word of Bahá'u'lláh, and were in utter contrast with the character and the outlook of history as the people of the West saw them. God's Will was the ruling force in the Bible as man's will dominates the direction of events in the Western mind.

It would have been easy and natural for 'Abdu'l-Bahá in the circumstances to have challenged the Western fallacy, exposed its error, developed an argument brilliant and overpowering to emphasize the agreement of His teaching with that of the Bible, and the hollowness of the Western expectation of a man-made kingdom and of materialistic hegemony of one race over others. But 'Abdu'l-Bahá did nothing of the kind. The great ideal which He held before His audiences was at all times and places one and the same: Unity Through Love. His *Paris Talks* are full throughout of a spiritual wisdom, a spontaneous warmth of heart and sweetness and winning tenderness that would be hard to match in the world's

revealed religious literature. His first public address was
delivered in a Christian Church in London[1]. He said,

*"This is a new cycle of human power. All the horizons of the
world are luminous, and the world will become indeed as a
garden and a paradise. . . . The gift of God to this enlightened
age is the knowledge of the oneness of mankind and of the
fundamental oneness of religion. Wars shall cease between
nations, and by the will of God the Most Great Peace shall
come . . ."*

This truth of a new dawning of power in the
world became the master thought of all His speeches
throughout His work in the West. In America, however,
He addressed the Americans particularly as Christians
and made an appeal to them not to be listeners only but to
become the reapers whom Christ had prophesied would
arise in His harvest day. He sought not only to instruct
and illumine the minds of His audience but to awaken in
them the power of spirituality and enthusiasm which
would overcome the materialism that infected mankind
and would develop in them a new loving spirituality
which would enable His message to get home to their
hearts.

He presented a new picture of Christ in contrast to the
Christ of orthodoxy, of sect and schism and dogma; one
which showed that Christ's real purpose was to unite
human hearts with the power of Divine love; such a
Christ as none had really conceived, eager, vigorous,
bringing together people of all sorts and kinds and races
and nations and overwhelming the prejudices and

[1] City Temple, Sept. 15th, 1911.

traditions which separated them. The natural force of His own warm, buoyant, loving nature gave power and reality to His presentation so that He was able to reveal a new Christ such as the people had never realized.

His American addresses open on a note of joy, of spontaneous abounding happiness and gratification at His meeting so many radiant hearts ready to listen to the Message which, in spite of His old age and imperfect health, He had come so far to give them. Only love from God and them would have brought Him. Heart and soul 'Abdu'l-Bahá radiated a triumphant confidence, clear and strong as can be, as He extolled the glory of Christ and Bahá'u'lláh, showing their closeness, the unity of their effort and their purpose.

His appeal was not to authority as was that of Bahá'u'lláh addressing the kings. He did not command. His appeal rather was to reason, to logic, to faith and to facts. He exposed the false hopes of the arrogant white race, not by disproof but by drawing in a quite natural manner a picture of the true antecedents of the Kingdom, showing it to be involved in the original creation of man.

He drew, in many aspects, a picture of the whole universe as governed by one unchanging law, as being created, ruled over and directed by one universal, independent, living Will. This great, out-working Spirit actuated the affairs and movements of all creatures in the world; it was the one Power which animated and dominated all existence. 'Abdu'l-Bahá spoke on this subject in an attitude of soul as logical as it was religious, as much in the mood of science as of faith. He treated the subject not only in a broad and general manner but in close detail. He traced, for example, the coursing of the atom through the kingdoms of nature—mineral, vegetable and animal—showing the changes that it assumes in its progress, through an activity not originating by itself. He showed that the one, living, independent Will of God which directed the transition of the atom directed likewise the movements which led mankind from one stage to another on its journey to the Kingdom. Thus He brought all nature into the same plane as man and showed, not only the oneness of mankind but of the whole universe—everything contributing, each in its own way—even if it be a preparatory way—towards the one great spiritual goal shown at its highest in the Kingdom of God.

He taught His auditors to meet the materialism of the day with reason and hard facts and He gave them Himself examples of how it could be done.

'Abdu'l-Bahá's first aim in His Western teaching was, as He says Himself, to create in the minds of His hearers capacity to understand and appreciate this great new Revelation. He did not wish them to be as the kings had shown themselves to be, so infected by the pride of man and the haughty scepticism of the age that they could not see the truth when it was put plainly and clearly before them. Christ, He reminded His auditors, had had the same difficulty and had spoken the parable of the sower to show it. 'Abdu'l-Bahá sought, as Christ in His day had done, to transform and spiritualize the very hearts and outlook of those to whom He spoke. Unless He could do this the exposure of one error in the minds of the people would only be followed on the next occasion by another error. No remedy was adequate except that of creating a real capacity in the human heart to see and love the truth. This and nothing less was the first and last aim of 'Abdu'l-Bahá.

His own personality was His greatest argument: He was so utterly sincere, so full Himself of truth and love that He had the power to convince (it would seem) even the most faithless.

In the second place His happy joyous way of presenting the argument appealed to those He spoke to and has its own penetrating power.

Those who knew 'Abdu'l-Bahá would say they could feel His overflowing love for mankind pouring from Him in great waves, and some have told how to sit beside Him in a motor-car was to feel oneself being charged by spiritual energy. What strikes many in reading His writings is that they possess a quality different from that which belongs to any human being. There is a cadence, a power in them which definitely comes from a higher world than that in which we live. It is natural, therefore, that His writings should be spoken of as Revelation. Yet He was human, not a Manifestation, and His scripture, though valid, has not the rank of the Revelation of a full Prophet. What explanation can there be of this except that the Holy Spirit is now in this Age of Truth touching men's souls with a higher degree of power than ever in the past. Our age has risen from the levels of the Kingdom of Man to the heights unapproached before of the Kingdom of God. 'Abdu'l-Bahá, the embodiment of every Bahá'í ideal, the incarnation of every Bahá'í virtue, presents man (revealed as made in the image of God) at a level higher than any we associate with man before.

Completing His Western tours, 'Abdu'l-Bahá, after nine months' ceaseless lecturing in the United States and Canada, reluctantly announced the imminent outbreak of the First World War and then went by Europe back to His home in

Haifa. He had, however, published translations of a number of Bahá'í Scriptures in America; organized Bahá'í communities in that country on a firm foundation; laid the foundation stone of a Bahá'í Temple in Wilmette on a site purchased at His direction. His efforts, however, to spread the Glad Tidings of the new Day far and wide found all too little response. After the outbreak of the First World War He tried to take the fullest advantage of the horror of war which the carnage had aroused by writing in and after 1916, a stirring summons to all Bahá'ís to arouse themselves and go forth through the length and breadth of the world to call all nations to the Kingdom of God. Once more He quoted the wonderful examples of the Apostles of Christ as a challenge to self-sacrifice. Fourteen of these letters constitute 'Abdu'l-Bahá's Divine Plan in which He detailed a vigorous and forthright programme for the carrying of the message of the New Day throughout the continents and the islands of the sea,—a plan fully worked out and likely to be in use for many generations to come. No great response was aroused among the Bahá'ís by this appeal, a fact which caused 'Abdu'l-Bahá poignant sorrow, compelling Him to realize how deep the suffering of the world would be which all His efforts had not been able to mitigate. Broken in heart He passed to His end three years after the War, foretelling that another war, fiercer than the last, would follow before long.

On His death the most deeply conceived and constructive of His works was published, known as *The Will and Testament of 'Abdu'l-Bahá*. It completed the great masterpiece of Bahá'u'lláh—His book of laws[1]—the two works together composing one complete and harmonious whole.

[1] *Kitáb-i-Aqdas*.

CHAPTER FIFTEEN

THE WILL AND TESTAMENT OF 'ABDU'L-BAHÁ

JESUS CHRIST said, *"My kingdom is not of this world,"* and Christian people have been inclined to think that pure religion is subjective and mystical only and has little or no connection with the organization of institutions or the making of laws or ordinances. This idea is quite alien to the New and the Old Testaments. The Kingdom of God is indeed a Kingdom, the ruler of which is not a philosopher nor a teacher, but a King with laws and subjects. The New Jerusalem which comes down from heaven and becomes the centre of the Kingdom represents the Law of God, while the distinctive function of the Lord of Hosts on earth is that "the government shall be upon his shoulder" and that He will administer "judgment and justice from henceforth, even forever."

The Will and Testament of 'Abdu'l-Bahá sets forth the administrative order by which this is to be accomplished, and, fathered by Bahá'u'lláh, provides the Bahá'í Faith with its historically unique feature—an administrative system based on the inviolable written Scripture, establishing and clearly defining the institutions, conferring authority, preventing schism, guarding the Revealed Word from adulteration, providing for its authoritative interpretation, and perpetuating the Divine guidance of the Lord of Hosts Himself.

"The creative energies released by the Law of

Bahá'u'lláh, permeating and evolving within the mind of 'Abdu'l-Bahá, have, by their very impact and close interaction, given birth to an Instrument which may be viewed as the Charter of the New World Order which is at once the glory and the promise of this most great Dispensation."[1]

The administrative institutions of the Kingdom, revealed by Bahá'u'lláh and defined and supplemented by 'Abdu'l-Bahá, include Houses of Justice at local, national and international levels. These bodies apply the Laws and Principles of Bahá'u'lláh to daily life, but the International House of Justice is specifically empowered to legislate on matters not provided for in the "Book," and is clearly stated by 'Abdu'l-Bahá to be *"under the care and protection of the Abhá Beauty, under the shelter and unerring guidance of ... the Exalted One ..."* Bahá'u'lláh Himself says of this institution, *"God will verily inspire them with whatsoever He willeth ..."* This is the legislative channel through which the rule of God will be perpetuated.

Nothing in the *Will and Testament* is more striking or more important than the immensity of the power conferred by 'Abdu'l-Bahá on the Guardian, and the note of personal admiration and affection with which the appointment of Shoghi Effendi, to be the Guardian, is characterized. Bahá'u'lláh had already foreshadowed this institution, but it was left to 'Abdu'l-Bahá, the Centre of the Covenant, to define it and establish it.

'Abdu'l-Bahá invokes *"salutation and praise, blessing and glory"* upon Shoghi Effendi, in whom is preserved the precious life blood of the two Prophets, the Báb and

[1] Shoghi Effendi, *The Dispensation of Bahá'u'lláh.*

Bahá'u'lláh, and describes him as *"the most wondrous, unique and priceless pearl that doth gleam from out the twin surging seas,"* for he is *"after my passing"* *"the Dayspring of Divine guidance."* *"He is the expounder of the Words of God and after him will succeed the first-born of his lineal descendants."* All must *"turn unto Shoghi Effendi,"* *"For he is, after 'Abdu'l-Bahá, the guardian of the Cause of God . . ."* *"He that obeyeth him not, hath not obeyed God; he that turneth away from him, hath turned away from God and he that denieth him hath denied the True One."* *"All must seek guidance and turn unto the Centre of the Cause and the House of Justice."*

Interpretation of the Word, which has always been the fertile source of schism in the past, is thus taken once and for all time, into His own hands by Bahá'u'lláh, and none other but His appointed Guardian, whom He guides, can fulfil this function. This is the secret of the unbreakable unity of the Bahá'í Faith and its entire and blessed lack of sects. *"The mighty stronghold shall remain impregnable and safe through obedience to him who is the guardian of the Cause of God."*

The effect of this appointment is to make the Guardian the source of continuing Divine guidance, and in such a way as to make it clear that although he would be the object of challenge, enmity and opposition, even of repudiation and denial, he would yet remain on the unassailable height of sure authority. The Guardian, in company with the Universal House of Justice, is under the express care and protection of Bahá'u'lláh and the unfailing guidance of the Báb. He thus must be taken as representing, while distinctly a human being, the nearest approach on earth to the Divine exaltation. When it is written that "the government shall be upon his shoulder" the reference can only be to the devolution by Bahá'u'lláh of supreme authority upon His divinely guided institutions, which thus embody His Covenant. This is the means—the Covenant—which the Lord of Hosts has designed to discharge His supreme mission, and the way in which God himself shall rule His people.

Commenting on the station of the Guardian and of Divine guidance which is so prominent a feature of the administrative order of Bahá'u'lláh, Shoghi Effendi writes:

"Exalted as is the position and vital as is the function of the institution of the Guardianship in the Administrative Order of Bahá'u'lláh, and staggering as must be the weight of responsibility which it carries, its importance must, whatever be the language of the Will, be in no wise over-emphasized. The Guardian of the Faith must not under any circumstances, and whatever his merits or his achievements, be exalted to the rank that will make him a co-sharer with 'Abdu'l-Bahá in the unique position which the Centre of the Covenant occupies—much less to the station exclusively ordained for the Manifestation of God. So grave a departure from the established tenets of our Faith is nothing short of open blasphemy. . . ."[1]

"No Guardian of the Faith, I feel it my solemn duty to place on record, can ever claim to be the perfect exemplar of the teachings of Bahá'u'lláh or the stainless mirror that reflects His light. Though overshadowed by the unfailing, the unerring protection of Bahá'u'lláh and of the Báb, and however much he may share with 'Abdu'l-Bahá the right and obligation to interpret the Bahá'í teachings, he

[1] *The Dispensation of Bahá'u'lláh.*

remains essentially human and cannot, if he wishes to remain faithful to his trust, arrogate to himself, under any pretence whatsoever, the rights, the privileges and prerogatives which Bahá'u'lláh has chosen to confer upon His Son. In the light of this truth to pray to the Guardian of the Faith, to address him as lord and master, to designate him as his holiness, to seek his benediction, to celebrate his birthday, or to commemorate any event associated with his life would be tantamount to a departure from those established truths that are enshrined within our beloved Faith. The fact that the Guardian has been specifically endowed with such power as he may need to reveal the purport and disclose the implications of the utterances of Bahá'u'lláh and of 'Abdu'l-Bahá does not necessarily confer upon him a station co-equal with those Whose words he is called upon to interpret."[1]

"Nor can the Bahá'í Administrative Order be dismissed as a hard and rigid system of unmitigated autocracy or as an idle imitation of any form of absolutistic ecclesiastical government, whether it be the Papacy, the Imamate or any other similar institution, for the obvious reason that upon the international elected representatives of the followers of Bahá'u'lláh has been conferred the exclusive right of legislating on matters not expressly revealed in the Bahá'í writings. Neither the Guardian of the Faith nor any institution apart from the International House of Justice can ever usurp this vital and essential power or encroach upon that sacred right. The abolition of professional priesthood with its accompanying sacraments of baptism, of communion and of confession of sins, the laws requiring the election by universal suffrage of all local, national, and international Houses

[1] ibid.

of Justice, the total absence of episcopal authority with its attendant privileges, corruptions and bureaucratic tendencies, are further evidences of the non-autocratic character of the Bahá'í Administrative Order and of its inclination to democratic methods in the administration of its affairs."[1]

These "twin pillars" of the Kingdom, unique in the religious history of the world, provide mankind with the fullest opportunity of ordering its own affairs through its elected representatives, whilst conferring upon it the supreme benefit, through the Divine guidance of the Guardian, of an inviolable constitution, the house built upon the rock of the unimpeachable, incorruptible Word of God Himself.

The close relationship between these two Divinely-guided institutions—the Guardianship and the International House of Justice—and the consultative method of Bahá'í administration are fully dealt with by 'Abdu'l-Bahá in His *Will and Testament* and elsewhere, though they form no part of this book. Suffice it to say that the guidance bestowed upon the House of Justice does not descend to the personal members, while the guidance bestowed upon the Guardian is personal to the holder of the office, the "*Sign of God*," the "*Dayspring of Divine guidance*," the "*Interpreter of the Word of God*."

Thus does the Prophetic cycle come to its end with the appearance of the Kingdom, conceived, established and governed by God. The age of fulfilment now opens when countless generations, never bereft of Divine guidance, upraised and loved by those Prophets Whom the Most High will, in His mercy, eternally send down, will pursue an ever-advancing civilization to the full development of man and the greater glory of God.

[1] ibid.

CHAPTER SIXTEEN

THE KINGDOM ON EARTH

WHATEVER the conception of the Kingdom of God at the end of the nineteenth century, it certainly did not hold before Christians the same supreme objective of prayer or aspiration which Christ had commanded in the Lord's Prayer. It was rather the Kingdom of Man than that of God—not of all men but of one race only and of certain members of that race who had achieved for themselves supremacy over the others. It would mean a world-wide Church, the domination of the white man, of white man's civilization, and it contemplated the perpetuation of an ever-increasing trade.

'Abdu'l-Bahá's picture, painted in full length and glowing colour in His Western addresses, was different indeed. He saw the coming of the Kingdom as the opening of the treasuries of heaven,—as the throwing wide of God's gates on splendours and glories hitherto beyond the reach of human imagination. So far were they from being a divine after-thought that they were, in fact, the originating motive of all creation, prepared before the foundation of the world. All the experiences of the whole human race, all the guidance and the education which the great Prophets had brought, all had been designed for and had led up to the human preparation for the Kingdom. Now, when the Prophets had completed their preliminary lessons and mankind was ready to attain maturity, God put forth His hand of power and sent the Lord of Hosts to release yet further spiritual energies and to establish at last the Kingdom of God on earth.

It was inevitable that the Kingdom of God, so foreseen and so established, should be built into a vast system in which the spiritual and material should be closely conjoined. Such a system has been provided by the Manifestation Himself and made more perfect in all respects than any previous form of government or administration. Of it Bahá'u'lláh wrote, *"Mankind's ordered life hath been revolutionized through the agency of this unique, this wondrous System—the like of which mortal eyes have never witnessed."*

Probably there is no description which so tersely and clearly gives the distinctive character of the oneness of mankind and the pattern of the Kingdom of God as the following paragraphs from Shoghi Effendi's *The Unfoldment of World Civilization.*

"Unification of the whole of mankind is the hall-mark of the stage which human society is now approaching. Unity of family, of tribe, of city state, and nation have been successively attempted and fully established. World unity is the goal towards which a harassed humanity is striving. . . .

"The unity of the human race, as envisaged by Bahá'u'lláh, implies the establishment of a world commonwealth in which all nations, races, creeds and classes are closely and permanently united, and in which the autonomy of its state members and the personal freedom and initiative of the individuals that compose them are definitely and completely safeguarded. This commonwealth must, as far as we can visualize it, consist of a world legislature, whose members will, as the trustees of the whole of mankind, ultimately control the entire resources of all the component nations, and will enact such laws as shall be required to regulate the life, satisfy the needs and adjust the relationships of all races and peoples. A world executive, backed by an international Force, will carry out the decisions arrived at, and apply the laws enacted by, this world legislature, and will safeguard the organic unity of the whole commonwealth. A world tribunal will adjudicate and deliver its compulsory and final verdict in all and any disputes that may arise between the various elements constituting this universal system. A mechanism of world inter-communication will be devised, embracing the whole planet, freed from national hindrances and restrictions, and functioning with marvellous swiftness and perfect regularity. A world metropolis will act as the nerve centre of a world civilization, the focus towards which the unifying forces of life will converge and from which its energizing influences will radiate. A world language will either be invented or chosen from among the existing languages and will be taught in the schools of all the federated nations as an auxiliary to their mother tongue. A world script, a world literature, a uniform and universal system of currency, of weights and measures, will simplify and facilitate intercourse and understanding among the nations and races of mankind. In such a world society, science and religion, the two most potent forces in human life, will be reconciled, will co-operate and will harmoniously develop. The press will, under such a system, while giving full scope to the expression of the diversified views and convictions of mankind, cease to be mischievously manipulated by vested interests, whether private or public, and will be liberated from the influence of contending governments and peoples. The economic resources of the world will be organized, its sources of raw materials will be tapped and fully utilized, its markets will be co-ordinated and developed, and the distribution of its products will be equitably regulated.

"National rivalries, hatreds, and intrigues will cease, and racial animosity and prejudice will be replaced by racial amity, understanding and co-operation. The causes of religious strife will be permanently removed, economic barriers and restrictions will be completely abolished, and the inordinate distinction between classes will be obliterated. Destitution on the one hand, and gross accumulation of ownership on the other, will disappear. The enormous energy dissipated and wasted on war, whether economic or political, will be consecrated to such ends as will extend the range of human inventions and technical development, to the increase of the productivity of mankind, to the extermination of disease, to the extension of scientific research, to the raising of the standard of physical health, to the sharpening and refinement of the human brain, to the exploitation of the unused and unsuspected resources of the planet, to the prolongation of human life, and to the furtherance of any other agency that can stimulate the intellectual, the moral, and spiritual life of the entire human race.

"A world federal system, ruling the whole earth and exercising unchallengeable authority over its unimaginably vast resources, blending and embodying the ideals of both the East and the West, liberated from the curse of war and its miseries, and bent on the exploitation of all the available resources of energy on the surface of the planet, a system in which Force is made the servant of Justice, whose life is sustained by its universal recognition of one God and by its allegiance to one common Revelation —such is the goal towards which humanity, impelled by the unifying forces of life, is moving."

The establishment of this Divine, yet earthly Kingdom, had always been associated, both in the Bible narrative and in its prophecies, with the Holy Land, which has become the home of the Bahá'í Faith. This has not been through its own act, so that none can say it deliberately caused fulfilment of the prophecies, but by the act of its enemies, the Sháh and the Sultán, who, in 1868, brought Bahá'u'lláh, a Persian born in Ṭihrán, as a prisoner and an exile to 'Akká. That city and its neighbourhood, especially Mount Carmel, has since become the most sacred spot in the Bahá'í world.

Bahá'u'lláh was endowed with the creative power to regenerate the whole of humanity and unify it in a single spiritual organism—a spiritual unity which was envisaged by God from the beginning and had never till now been made a reality—and it is a remarkable fact that through the agency of this Order, as yet but embryonic, the Faith of Bahá'u'lláh has succeeded in preserving its unity and integrity, both in thought and in action during the most critical periods of its Heroic and Formative ages. That such a test suddenly facing, as it did on the death of 'Abdu'l-Bahá, a community of hundreds of thousands of believers of all classes, nations, races and traditions should be so successfully met, is an achievement almost incredible. Yet it is early evidence of the indubitable truth that every human being has an equal right with every other to a place in the Kingdom, which will need the participation of all to make a perfect mirror reflecting the full splendours of the Holy Spirit.

Hitherto mankind has been divided into two sections— the good and the bad, the faithful and the infidel, the elect and the lost,—but now with the coming of the Kingdom all are to be treated and counted as one, and 'Abdu'l-Bahá insisted that all men from now on should treat each other so. What now appears plain to one who approaches this divine Order is that Bahá'u'lláh has provided all the means for mankind's preservation in the fortress of unity, and leads and guides man along the path to the good-pleasure of God Who *"cherisheth in His heart the desire of beholding the entire human race as one soul and one body."*

Thus, the vast concourse of God's citizens at the inception of His Kingdom have before them the prospect of building a universal World Commonwealth which will develop in the fullness of time into a world spiritual civilization. Of this great day 'Abdu'l-Bahá has written, gathering up all the threads of the past, *"One of the great events which is to occur in the Day of the manifestation of that incomparable Branch is the hoisting of the Standard of God among all nations. By this is meant that all nations and kindreds will be gathered together under the shadow of this Divine Banner, which is no other than the Lordly Branch itself, and will become a single nation. Religious and sectarian antagonism, the hostility of races and peoples, and differences among nations, will be eliminated. All men will adhere to one religion, will have one common faith, will be blended into one race and become a single people. All will dwell in one common fatherland, which is the planet itself."*

It is the ancient vision coming true at last, the glorious Kingdom of hope and faith descending from heaven to encompass all the earth.

> "And I saw a new heaven and a new earth: for the first heaven and the first earth were passed away; and there was no more sea. And I John saw the holy city, new Jerusalem, coming down from God out of heaven, prepared as a bride adorned for her husband. And I heard a great voice out of heaven, saying, Behold, the tabernacle of God is with men, and he will dwell with them, and they shall be his people, and God himself shall be with them, and be their God. And God shall wipe away all tears from their eyes; and there shall be no more death, neither sorrow, nor crying, neither shall there be any more pain: for the former things are passed away." (*Rev.* xxi)

EPILOGUE

When no heed was given to Bahá'u'lláh's Declaration that His prophethood was the return of Christ, when His appeal for the examination of His Cause and the redress of cruel wrongs inflicted on Him was ignored; when no one regarded His forecast, so forcefully and so fully presented, that a new Dawn had broken, a New Age had come (new in a spiritual sense, in a moral sense, in an intellectual sense), an Age which would bring a new outlook and new concepts, an Age of Divine Judgment, in which tyranny would be thrown down, the rights of the people asserted, and in which the social structure of the human race would be changed; when no attention was paid to the vision He opened, to the opportunities He offered, to the bold challenge which He had from prison flung before the mighty ones of the world; then alas! the Churches as the years went by found themselves caught into a current which bore them irresistibly downward at an ever increasing speed and which at the end of eight decades was still to be bearing them down to lower and yet lower levels in their political standing, in their moral influence, in their intellectual prestige, in their social authority, in their numbers and their financial resources, in the popular estimate of the relevancy and the reality of the religion which they taught and even in the vigour and unanimity of their own witness to the basic truth upon which the Church itself had been founded.

No comparable period of deterioration is to be found in the long records of the Christian Faith. In all the vicissitudes of fifteen eventful centuries (and they were many); in all the misfortunes, the mistakes, the failures and the humiliations in which from time to time the Church was involved, no such catastrophic decline is to be traced. The sovereignty which the Church had wielded in the Middle Ages had indeed by the nineteenth century become in Western Europe a thing of the past; but the diminution had been gradual and moderate. The loss suffered during the previous eight hundred years can hardly be compared with the vital damage inflicted during the last eighty.

In past crises the foundations of faith and of western society were not shaken; hope remained dominant, and from tradition and memory men drew inspiration. Society remained Christian and to that extent unified. But now the very foundations have gone. Reverence and restraint are no more. The heights of human nature are closed: its depths opened. Substitute systems of ethics, man-made and man-regarding, are invented, dethroning conscience. The dignity of reason and of knowledge is denied: truth itself is impugned.

The story of this calamitous decline is well known to all, and its outstanding features can be briefly summarized.

In the year 1870, not long after the despatch of Bahá'u'lláh's Tablet to his Holiness, the Pope was through King Victor Emmanuel's seizure of Rome deprived by force of virtually the whole of that temporal power which Bahá'u'lláh had advised him to renounce voluntarily. His formal acknowledgment of the Kingdom of Italy by the recent Lateran Treaty sealed this resignation of sovereignty.

The fall of the Napoleonic Empire was followed in

France by a wave of anti-clericalism which led to a complete separation of the Roman Catholic Church from the State, the secularization of education, and the suppression and dispersal of the religious orders.

In Spain, the monarchy which for so long had been in Christendom the great champion of the Roman Church was overthrown and the State secularized.

The dismemberment of the Austro-Hungarian monarchy caused the disappearance both of the last remnant of the Holy Roman Empire and of the most powerful political unit that gave to the Roman Church its spiritual and financial support.

In Soviet Russia an organized assault directed against the Greek Orthodox Church, against Christianity, and against religion, disestablished that church, massacred vast numbers of its hundred million members, stripped it of its six and a half million acres of property, pulled down, closed or perverted to secular uses countless thousands of places of worship and by "a five-year plan of godlessness" sought to eradicate all religion from the hearts of the people.

In every land and in all branches of the Christian Church, even where there was no system of Establishment, the rising power of nationalism continually made churches more and more subservient to the interests and the opinions of the State—a tendency brought into strong relief and notoriety in the first world war.

The gradual decay of the intellectual prestige of religion in Europe had extended over many generations, but it was brought prominently before the public mind in the seventies of the last century, largely through the controversies which followed Tyndall's Belfast address in 1874. The character of this decay has been epitomized by Professor Whitehead, writing in 1926, thus:

"Religion is tending to degenerate into a decent formula wherewith to embellish a comfortable life. . . . For over two centuries, religion has been on the defensive, and on a weak defensive. The period has been one of unprecedented intellectual progress. In this way a series of novel situations has been produced for thought. Each such occasion has found the religious thinkers unprepared. Something which has been proclaimed to be vital has, finally, after struggle, distress and anathema been modified and otherwise interpreted. The next generation of religious apologists then congratulates the religious world on the deeper insight which has been gained. The result of the continued repetition of this undignified retreat during many generations has at last almost entirely destroyed the intellectual authority of religious thinkers. Consider this contrast; when Darwin or Einstein proclaims theories which modify our ideas, it is a triumph for science. We do not go about saying there is another defeat for science, because its old ideas have been abandoned. We know that another step of scientific insight has been gained."

The loss in the moral and spiritual field has been even more vital and conspicuous, especially of recent years. There is no need to enlarge upon the matter. The sickness at the heart of Christian life and thought which made these humiliations possible has been the decay of spirituality. Love for God, fear of God, trust in God's overruling providence and ceaseless care have been no longer active forces in the world. The religious thinkers find themselves baffled by the portents of the time: when men in disillusionment, in anguish and despair come to them for counsel, seek from them comfort, hope, some intelligible

idea as to what this cataclysm means and whence it came
and how it should be met, they are completely at a loss.
Though the Church for nineteen centuries has proclaimed,
and has enshrined in its creeds, the emphatic and repeated
promise of Christ that He would come again in power
and great glory to judge the earth, would exalt the
righteous and inaugurate the Kingdom of God among
mankind, yet they believe and teach that through all
these years of deepening tribulation no Hand has been
outstretched from heaven, no light of Guidance has been
shed upon the earth; that God has withheld from His
children in their deepest need His succour, His comfort
and His love; that Christ has utterly forgotten His
promise or is impotent to redeem it and has permitted
His universal Church to sink in ruin without evincing
the least small sign of His interest or His concern.

Meantime the Bahá'í Message has kindled once more
on earth the ancient fire of faith that Jesus kindled long
ago, the fire of spontaneous love for God and man, a
love that changes all life and longs to show itself in deeds
of devotion and of self-sacrifice even to death and
martyrdom. To them who have recognized Christ's voice
again in this Age has been given in renewed freshness and
beauty the vision of the Kingdom of God as Jesus and the
Book of Revelation gave it—the same vision, but clearer
now and on a larger scale and in more detail. A new
enthusiasm is theirs, a power that nothing can gainsay or
resist. Their words reach the hearts of men. With a courage,
a determination that only divine love could quicken or
support they have arisen in the face of ruthless persecution
to bear witness to their faith. Fearless, though compara-
tively few, weak in themselves but invincible in God's
Cause, they have now at the close of little over a hundred

years carried that Faith far and wide through the globe, entered well over two hundred and fifty countries, translated their literature into three hundred and fifty languages, gathered adherents from East and West, from many races, many nations, many creeds, many traditions, and have established themselves as a world-community, worshipping one God under one Name.

The Bahá'í Faith to-day presents the Christian Churches with the most tremendous challenge ever offered them in their long history: a challenge, and an opportunity. It is the plain duty of every earnest Christian in this illumined Age to investigate for himself with an open and fearless mind the purpose and the teachings of this Faith and to determine whether the collective centre for all the constructive forces of this time be not the Messenger from God, Bahá'u'lláh, He and no other; and whether the way to a better, kinder, happier world will not lie open as soon as we accept the Announcement our rulers rejected.

"O kings of the earth! He Who is the sovereign Lord of all is come. The Kingdom is God's, the omnipotent Protector, the Self-Subsisting. Worship none but God, and, with radiant hearts, lift up your faces unto your Lord, the Lord of all names. This is a Revelation to which whatever ye possess can never be compared, could ye but know it."

O, Christian believers! for your own sakes and for the sake of the Churches, for the sake of all mankind, for the sake of the Kingdom, cast away your conflicting dogmas and interpretations which have caused such disunity and led us to the verge of wholesale self-destruction. Recognize the age of Truth. Recognize Christ in the glory and power of the Father and, heart and soul, throw yourselves into His Cause.

*"It is my hope thy Church will come
under the heavenly Jerusalem."*

'ABDU'L-BAHÁ

Three books no sincere Christian would want to miss:

THE PROMISE OF ALL AGES

THE HEART OF THE GOSPEL

CHRIST AND BAHÁ'U'LLÁH

Townshend's sublime vision of human history as an epic written
by the finger of God.

The Promise of All Ages
by GEORGE TOWNSHEND

This book contains not only an argument but a story; a story of men of vision and action, the pioneers of a new era. Townshend depicts the history of humanity in terms of the unfolding of the Divine Plan, culminating in the establishment of the Kingdom of God on earth, when God Himself shall rule His people, His will shall prevail here as it does throughout the universe, and the earth shall be filled with His knowledge and radiant with His love.

184 pages

ISBN HC 0–85398–044–6
ISBN SC 0–85398–006–3

The Heart of the Gospel
by GEORGE TOWNSHEND

'What the early Christians did we can do. The opportunity given to them is repeated in our time. The same strength which was given to them may be claimed by us too. The civilisation into which they were born was cankered at the heart, and was dying of irreligion. They, because they loved God and were possessed with the knowledge of His truth, were endowed with power from on high to convert the world and to build by slow degrees a new social order more near than the old to the divine ideal. We, in a like emergency, are called on to undertake a like task.'

160 pages

ISBN Softcover 0–85398–020–9

George Townshend
by DAVID HOFMAN

The literary biography of the author of *The Promise of All Ages, The Heart of the Gospel,* and *Christ and Bahá'u'lláh,* by his publisher and literary executor. Townshend took as his mandate 'Abdu'l-Bahá's letter to him of 1920: 'It is my hope thy Church will come under the heavenly Jerusalem'. His story is fascinating and inspiring, covering his recognition of the new Revelation – the long-awaited Kingdom on earth promised by Christ – his striving to arouse his fellow churchmen to it, and his resignation of his high rank and Orders after forty years 'in order to be loyal to Christ as I know Him', willingly embracing the hardships and misunderstandings which that action entailed. He became one of the great figures of the Bahá'í Faith, and was among the first twelve to be appointed Hands of the Cause of God in their own lifetimes.

448 pages, 63 illustrations

ISBN 0–85398–126–4 Hardcover
ISBN 0–85398–127–2 Softcover

The Mission of Bahá'u'lláh *and other literary pieces*
by GEORGE TOWNSHEND

Essays, poems and meditations for those who seek a spiritual way of life.

160 pages

ISBN 0–85398–021–7 Hardcover